A Journey

to

Remember 1939-45

To:- Richard

With Best Wishes

From:- Jim Gonzales

A Journey

to

Remember 1939-45

THE DIARY OF A LIVERPOOL SOLDIER

BY

JAMES GONZALES

EDITED BY

W. R. COCKCROFT M.A.

ISBN 0 903348 49 7

Typeset and compiled by Print Origination Formby and
Books Unlimited (Nottm)
Printed and bound by Cromwell Press Ltd Melksham, Wilts

Dedication

I humbly dedicate this book to all those who made and completed
the journey and most particularly to those we left behind, also to

... ... my Mother who for over 5 years kept the home fires burning

... ... my brother Ray who served in the Merchant Navy

... ... my sister Joan who worked in the Royal Ordnance Factory

The Author James Gonzales soon after enlistment

Contents

Foreword

It is fortunate for future generations that James Gonzales ignored the rules against the keeping of diaries, and is so able to give us this vivid and moving account of his experiences with the Royal Army Ordnance Corps, his part of which became the Royal Electrical and Mechanical Engineers in 1942.

The long journey of the 5th Division by sea and road to the east of India (to meet a Japanese threat which never materialised), and back via the Persian Gulf and Iraq, showed that hardships and deaths are not only caused by the enemy. The Division then took a leading part in the invasions of Sicily and Italy, and the author gives a graphic account of the brave deeds of many of his comrades, and a modest one of his own part in the important task of keeping many different vehicles and machines in running order, which lead to his promotion to staff-sergeant.

The descriptions of battle are skilfully interwoven with those of the relaxation provided by ENSA, films and the best opera. They combine to give a convincing account of the way our soldiers supported each other in facing years of hardship and danger fighting for their country.

I hope this book will bring home to its younger readers the scale of the deeds and endurance of their fathers and grandfathers which enabled their decendants to live in freedom.

Kitchener

The Rt. Hon. Earl Kitchener of Khartoum
President of the 8th Army Veterens Association

Chapter One

Liverpool Life, 1939

My father was a merchant seaman of Spanish decent and I spent the first decades of my life, happily in Walton, a suburb of the world famous English seaport of Liverpool. As a youth I was aware of its reputation as the transit town for thousands of European and Irish immigrants who had sailed into the River Mersey to eagerly await further passage to a new life in the Americas. Countless thousands of these travellers had often desperately sought the means of acquiring the fastest route by sea out of the port. Little did I realise in 1939, at the age of 24 years that I too would be reluctantly plucked by fate and thrust into a world-wide drama that would leave countless thousands condemned to the irrepressible violence, maiming, suffering and degradation of war.

I first became aware of the clock that began to tick its way towards my appointments with uncontrollable fate on the morning of the 1st September 1939. When the impasse between Britain and Germany became clearly defined, war was commonly talked about as being inevitable. Precautions against possible enemy aircraft bombing raids were soon brought into effect. The chief of these I remembered was the Blackout measures introduced not only on Merseyside but also throughout the entire United Kingdom. All the homes in my neighbourhood had the insides of their windows covered with heavy black material that was sealed by adhesive tape. Such measures, which were also stringently applied to local factories and businesses, were to prevent any light in the hours of darkness becoming visible to enemy aircraft.

Two days later at 11 o'clock on the morning of the 3rd September, the stunning announcement that war had been

Sinking of the Athenia

declared was heard on the radio. The reality of this terse declaration was sickeningly brought home to all in our neighbourhood when we heard that the liner S.S. Athenia – which had left Liverpool with some 1500 men, women and children on board – was sunk by enemy 'U' boat submariners off the coast of Scotland. Its destination had been New York.

The next in our growing litany of deprivations occurred the following day when all our local cinemas were closed to the public. This meant that our habit of coming home from work, having a hurried meal and then dashing out to the first performance at the local cinema, or 'picture house', was abruptly curtailed. Our favourite film stars, such as John Wayne, Greta Garbo, Clark Gable, Fred Astaire, Ginger Rogers, Humphrey Bogart, Bob Hope and Bing Crosby to name just a few, were, for the foreseeable future, no longer able to project their individual magical spell of entertainment over us. In stark contrast my family and I – like almost everyone in our street – became accustomed to seat themselves around the wireless, or 'radio', for the six o'clock news bulletin. In my own household I clearly remember my mother sitting with my sister, my brother and myself to await details of the 'latest' events which had occurred.

Within a few days from the announcement of war the daily

humdrum and happy patterns in our life style were altered as if by decree. At that time I was employed as a meter inspector in the Liverpool Corporation Electrical Supply Department. Like others in the heart of the City, our office was transferred overnight to a less dangerous site on the outskirts – to 'rural' Woolton.

Then we had a small change of fortune. On the 15th September all the local cinemas and theatres were re-opened in an attempt to raise morale. 'Thank goodness', was a common reaction as some also began to talk in terms that suggested we had only experienced a 'Phoney War'. By this time, however, air-raid sirens had been installed near most public places and when they were sounded we were 'herded out' of any place of entertainment. If we heard their woeful wail whilst riding on a tram-car our journey was abruptly brought to a halt. On numerous occasions I remembered quickly scrambling from one of the maroon and cream trams and running through the city streets to seek shelter. In our back garden we had an 'Anderson' air raid shelter, (named after the Home Secretary) used by our family extensively. The shelter was made with curved corrugated

Air raid shelter, 18 Graylands Rd

metal sheets. In many homes with rear gardens the shelters were sunk about five to six feet below ground level. Inside each there was accommodation in the small compartments for about six people. The shrill continuous tone from the sirens the ('All-Clear' signal) brought a collective sigh of relief from all of their inmates when they would emerge to survey the outcome of the air raid.

Three days after the lifting of the curfew on cinemas and theatres we were again starkly reminded of the seriousness of our position when we heard a report over the radio that the Aircraft Carrier 'Courageous' had been sunk and had become the second major shipping casualty of the war. We took this particularly hard because of our experiences of seeing many similar vessels on the River Mersey. Many of these had been designed and built in the world famous Cammell Laird Shipbuilding Yards which were sited just three miles across the River Mersey in Birkenhead..

Little by little the ease and comfort of life in peace time was replaced by an edginess and uneasiness that worsened in an almost imperceptible way. Early in October, as winter beckoned, a thunderstorm broke over the North West of England and it was so violent that my family and I feared that an enemy bombing-raid had commenced. Eight 'barrage balloons', (used as deterrents to bombers using low flying tactics to pin point their targets,) were brought down in this storm but this was an anti-climax for what was to follow.

We moved uneasily into the festive season which became, unknown to me at the time, the last that I was to enjoy in the bosom of my family for many years With psychological cunning the enemy intruded upon any would-be hopes we might subconsciously have nurtured for the New Year of 1940. After the latent joy of muted traditional celebrations our first genuine air-raid occurred on the 1st January. I spent the night with members of my family in the cellar of the house of one of our relations listening to, and feeling the regular shudder of the bombs that fell nearby. After the 'all clear' was sounded I walked

home and was appalled to see the damage incurred to a variety
of shops in Breck Road.

After this baptism of Fire we were submitted to many more
air-raids – each one as breathtaking and savage in its intent as the
first. Our down-turn in fortune seemed to be symbolised by the
deterioration in weather conditions that crept in by mid January.
We were forced to endure the coldest winter for fifty years as
temperatures fell as low as 14º F. When heavy snowfalls and
blinding blizzards followed, most road vehicles, including the
usually reliable tramcars, were brought to a standstill. We felt like
sitting ducks as depths of snow, sometimes up to two feet high,
restricted our movement in and around 'town'. Though we
usually dismissed any talk of our situation as getting worse we
could not help thinking that the bad weather was an omen about

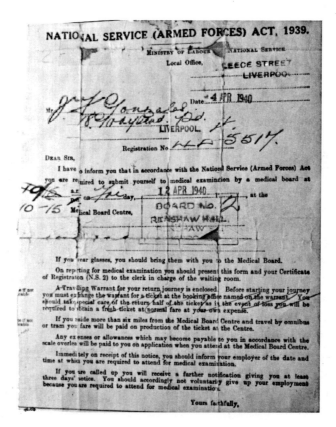

Calling up papers

our ill-fated future. Could matters get worse? I had to wait several months in something of a suspended state before I received what appeared to me to be an answer.

By mid winter, the 4th February, a thaw in the weather began to set in and I mistakenly felt that some pattern of respite and normality had returned to my life. With the onset of Spring that year a further shock for me was to follow. On the 6th April, a month noted for the playing of foolish tricks, I was handed a buff-coloured envelope bearing my name. Apprehensively opening the envelope I found papers with orders, under the National Services Act, 1939, for me to report for an Armed Forces' medical at Liverpool's Renshaw Hall. Within a week after the examination I was notified that I was A1, fit for service. From this point onwards my family constantly wondered when I might leave them and where I was bound for.

Within the next few months I mentally felt more like C3 as my

Medical Report

own personal morale seemed to ebb and flow. Firstly, time seemed to drag as more air-raids had to be endured. On 28th April I spent the entire night with my family in one of the district's barren shelters. When we emerged we were

The King and Queen driving along Queens Drive, Walton

confronted by serious damage to some houses and shops in the nearby Anfield district of the City – the home of Liverpool Association Football Club. Three days later, probably to lift our flagging spirits, His Majesty King George V1 and the Queen visited Liverpool. By this time our local recreational grounds of Walton Park boasted the somewhat incongruous attraction of the new Ack Ack anti-aircraft guns which seemed to inject a new

Anti-aircraft gun in Walton Park

confidence into all our neighbours. When their Majesties were driven through our neighbourhood along the aptly named Queen's Drive they were accompanied by a leading regiment of soldiers. Little did I realise as I stood in a cheering crowd that lined the route that I would later meet His Majesty at an inspection parade in Oakley Park – prior to embarking with my military unit on the long voyage to India.

My family's usual delight in the coming of springtime and its longer hours of daylight and greater warmth was abruptly curtailed by the chilling news of the 10th May. It was then that we learned that our European neighbouring countries, Holland and Belgium had been invaded by the German armed forces. One month later, on the 10th June, Italy under its fascist supremo Benito Mussolini sided with Hitler and also declared war on the Allied powers.

On the so called 'unlucky' day of that month, 13th June, my life changed irrevocably. I received my second set of 'call-up' papers. These bore orders that I had to undertake active service in the British Army – as a 'gunner' in the 39th Signal Training Regiment

2 pages of Pay Book

SOLDIER'S PAY BOOK (ACTIVE SERVICE)
ARMY BOOK 64 (PART II)

Army Number *988195*

Surname (block letters) *GONZALES J*

Christian Names in full *JAMES FREDERICK*

....

Regiment or Corps..
(TITLE OF UNIT MUST NOT BE ENTERED.)

Instructions to Soldier

1. You will produce this book whenever you require an advance of cash on account, or when instructed to do so.
2. You will give a receipt, on the acquittance roll of the Officer paying you, for all cash advances made to you. The Officer making the payment will sign the corresponding entry in this book on the page for cash payments.
3. You will make no entries in this book, except to sign your name and enter your Army number on pages 7, 9, 11 and 13.
4. Should you lose your book you will at once report the loss to your Commanding Officer, when a new book will be issued to you, but it must be understood that no pay can be issued in respect of the period before the date on which you report your loss, until your balance has been ascertained from the Paymaster.
5. You should read carefully the information on pages 1, 2 and 3.

Pay Book details

of the Royal Artillery. My spirits were initially raised by the knowledge that I had been called to serve my King and Country. In less than a week I was called upon to sacrifice my family life and my friends. My civilian career had disappeared overnight. As I boarded the number 44 tramcar near my home, on the 20th of that month, hundreds of happy home memories swept through my mind. After arriving in the City Centre amidst the great office buildings of Moorfields I anxiously made my way to Exchange Station to take the 9am. steam-train to the scenic Yorkshire holiday resort of Scarborough.

Within a short time of my arrival I had reported to the reception desk at the prestigious Grand Hotel. Any doubts that I

Grand Hotel, Scarborough

might have mistakenly had that I was to be sent for officer training were quickly dispelled. A non-commissioned officer informed me that I would be in 'A battery'. This left me a little puzzled because the term to me at that moment in time simply referred to the black box of electrical energy under a motor vehicle's bonnet. Before I could make further inquiries about this I was taken to my hotel quarters. These consisted of a double-bedded room that overlooked the perilous North Sea. I allowed myself the luxury of thinking at the time "mm, a room with a view overlooking the sea, hey!" Little did I know at that point in time that I was to be put through a thoroughly exhausting physical exercise routine just outside the hotel on the following morning. Sergeant Powers, a P.T. instructor was to become my very own 'iron fist in the velvet glove' with the ability to make or break all his new charges in that unassuming seaside town.

When I first entered 'my' bedroom I tentatively carried with me my new army personal kit bag. On this was my army service number 988195. The kit had been drawn from the Central Stores of the Royal Artillery's Camp, on the site of the 'Grand'. I gingerly placed the bag on the single bed at the left hand side of the room.

At that moment I turned in surprise to see another of the King's recruits enter the room with his full-kit. He walked to the other bed and placed his baggage upon it. Without a second thought he offered his hand for the traditional hand shake as he announced himself to be Bill Duckworth from Darwen, Lancashire. This young man, I later discovered, had been an Insurance's Firm representative in civilian life. His goodwill gesture marked the beginning of a friendship that was to last throughout the War and indeed for several decades after it. We were both later to reflect over many years on those initial shocks we were to undergo in our first introduction to the army – in Squad 33. The latter consisted of a training group which varied at times between 15 and 20 men.

In this, the season of Summer, many of our group had traditionally anticipated the joy and freedom of a small family holiday. Not only was this freedom now to be sacrificed but so were a host of other freedoms previously taken for granted. This was a limbo of regimentation which we had to endure for many years ahead. In the last week in June, on the 24th and 25th, respectively we lost our last vestiges of civilian life. We handed over our everyday clothing in exchange for army kit and the appropriate accessories. Next we were kitted out with a full army uniform. To the latter was added a ground sheet, two boot brushes, anti-gas ointment, a shaving brush and a razor, kit-bag, valise, belt and braces, and a pair of puttees, (a cloth strip which wound around the base of the trousers and top of the boots). Before our daily army routine began we were also sent to the Brigade's Armoury to each collect a Lee Enfield rifle.

On 25th June we began a daily routine that lasted for a fortnight. At a somewhat early hour each morning we began Physical Training Exercises on the seashore in front of the Grand. A Captain Hall inspected our bedrooms to ensure that our kit and accessories were laid out in the correct manner. Failure in any matter almost guaranteed you would be 'put on Jankers' which engaged you in some loathsome duty such as potato peeling or floor moppings. In the afternoons we were chiefly engaged in rifle drill until standard commands, such as stand to attention,

Nostell Priory near Wakefield

slope arms, present arms, right dress, stand easy and stand at ease – became second nature to us.

By the second week in July we had moved on from our temporary seaside base to Nostell Priory. This magnificent, grand Georgian style country home was situated in wooded rural surroundings near Wakefield. It fell to us not to live within the splendour of the Priory itself but within the canvas 'walls' of our Bell tents! Here we continued to train rigorously for three consecutive days so that by 12th July we had reached operational standards. At this point we were inspected, between 8am. and 9.30am., by our Lieutenant Colonel Commanding Officer. The following day, which for me became the unlucky thirteenth I experienced my first set-back in my new army career. Whilst exercising in the Priory's gymnasium I jumped from the wall-bars to the floor only to feel the squad member behind me accidentally thrust one of his feet into the small of my back. Reeling in pain and after being examined by the site medical officer I was assigned to light duties for the rest of the week. This brought my army service to just over one calendar month and my 'passing out', on 26th July, from 'A' Battery. With this achievement behind me I hurriedly made my way back to

Liverpool for 48 hours freedom in civilian life. To meet my mother and the members of family again was a never to be forgotten tonic.

Shortly after I returned from leave, on 29th July, I was ordered to move to B Battery. I attended lectures on the care and maintenance of Brigade Vehicles and was given driving tuition before I became one of their first 'casualties' in the war. On the 3rd August the pain I had endured since my nasty gymnastic experience became unbearable. The Medical Officer who initially suspected me to be a malingerer sent me to Pinderfield Hospital in Wakefield for an X-ray. Here my trouble was diagnosed as being three small fractures at the base of my spine. When these were reported to our Medical Officer, he profusely apologised for not sending me to hospital earlier. After a period of rest I was re-assigned to driving lessons with one Sergeant Hillman. At first I was instructed in the use of a 1936 Wolesely. Later, on 8th August. I progressed to the more exciting 'rough riding' of BSA and Norton motor-cycles in old quarries and through ditches and other water filled tracks.

Mid August witnessed a more realistic acclimatisation to battle conditions after an Invasion Alert was sounded in the early hours of 17th of that month. Fortunately the attack did not occur and by 28th I was ready for a further 48 hours leave. Again I was pleased to be the centre of attention as my family greeted me and enthusiastically welcomed me home with a special party.

When I returned to Wakefield I continued with my course of lectures and driving instructions for both motor cars and motor-cycles. Within a week of my return I was sent into Leeds where I successfully undertook a driving test. A week later, on 7th September, I passed 'with merit' from B Battery to C. At another large house on a country estate at nearby Bretton Park, I was trained in the use of Morse Code on the 'buzzer and lamp routine'. As I entered or left the establishment I had to give the appropriate pass words to continue on my way.

From this time onwards the Autumn and Winter of 1940

seemed to pass quickly as I became accustomed to a soldier's life and the constraints and trials that it brought with it. A second Invasion Alert was implemented which lasted from 11.30pm. on the 8th September to 4am. on the 9th. In the evening we were invited to the Town Institute where we thoroughly enjoyed a concert held especially for us. Before September expired, however, we had two pieces of bad news to contend with. On the 23rd of that month we heard that a British ship had been sunk but we were not given any further details. Two days later one of our Hampden Bomber aircraft crashed close to the village of Haig in Bretton Park there were three casualties. We were placed on guard duty.

The following month, on 2nd October, we accepted an invitation to an Artillery Ball in Wakefield. Not being very interested in dancing I attended the occasion to enjoy the social chatter but did little dancing myself. No matter how much we relaxed I was always fearful of the continuing air-raids over my home in Liverpool. In the middle of the month, on 13th, I 'passed out' from B Battery but had to undertake a fire piquet duty that very night watching for incendiary bombs as we were placed on alert for a possible enemy air-raid.

Two weeks later I was given seven days leave and found this break particularly welcome after our previous camp tensions. Alas there was to be 'no peace for the wicked' or so it seemed as on the first night of my home leave, there was a heavy air-raid which lasted from 7pm. to 4am. During this period and during the following night I spent my time in the local air-raid shelter. We occupied ourselves by talking, singing or listening to a portable battery-operated radio. Fortunately, our friends and neighbours always managed to bring plenty of refreshments for us to share. When we eventually emerged we were dismayed to find that many casualties had been incurred and that a frightening amount of damage to local property had occurred.

It was with a strange sense of 'relief' that I returned to my army camp. Here I was given the news that I was to be transferred, on Guy Fawkes Night, 5th November, to the Depot Battery. Our

Training Centre Croydon (author top left)

routines of rifle drill and Bren Gun drill on a special range were to be intensified. Unlike our rifles the Bren was an automatic gun to be found on the heavily protected ranges. When firing, the gun had to be firmly placed against the shoulder because considerable pressure from its hefty recoil action was exerted when it was fired. I mastered the technique for using it but my relatively trouble-free life in this pleasant rural district of Yorkshire was soon to end.

As the season of Advent advanced, I was posted, on 14th December, to the South East London Institute in Lewisham. The experience of aerial bombardment in Liverpool was to help me through this particularly strenuous time. I was to undertake a special two month course in electrical engineering but my duties were not confined to the daytime lectures and practical sessions. Once billeted I, together with about another fifteen to twenty recruits also living there, was expected to undertake fire piquet duties each night. Before successfully completing the first part of the course I assisted in the precautions drawn up to cope with the many incendiary bombs that were dropped into the district. For

Divisional Badges

part two of the course I was transferred to the Croydon Technical Training College.

The latter period was to be the last time of duty in the war that I was not engaged on active duty. On 2nd April 1941 I was posted to join the Light Aid Detachment of the Ninety Second Field Regiment Royal Artillery. This I came to realise was part of the British Fifth Division, which was based in the North of England. It came under Western Command and had its headquarters at Knutsford.

Whilst it was pleasant to feel that I had moved nearer 'home' we were soon thrust into a dreadfully cold weather spell, and I came to realise just how much lower temperatures could fall in the North of the England than in the South. In mid April, about the 15th and 16th, the Fifth Division had planned to move to the sandy coastal shores off Formby, north of Liverpool, for a 'practice battle'. This was to involve a crossing in moonlight over the River Alt which flowed into the Irish Sea. This in turn it was felt would help the Royal Engineers gain practical experience in bridge building operations across a river at night.

It was my duty in L.A.D. to attend to all vehicle electrical components, for repairs and maintenance, sometimes in very arduous and frightening situations. Our L.A.D. unit was attached to the Fifteenth Infantry Brigade which included the 365, 368 and 467 Battery's, and incorporated some famous Battalions – The First Green Howard's, the First Kings Own Yorkshire Light Infantry – and others. Though our L.A.D. was initially incorporated in the Royal Ordnance Corps, it was later transferred, in 1942, to the newly formed Royal Electrical and Mechanical Engineers unit.

Three days before we were due to take part in this river crossing exercise it was learned that the 15th Infantry Brigade would have to pull out and move instead to Northern Ireland. Leaving shortly after this information was received we headed north to take the main road beyond Carlisle to Stranraer in Scotland. Once there we boarded ships to cross for Larne over a stretch of water in the Irish Sea that was infamous for the activity of enemy submarines or U boats. Having arrived without incident we headed towards our new divisional headquarters at Armagh. It fell to us to carry out routine army vehicle maintenance or repairs in the border country around Omagh – Newtown Stewart.

My period of active service in Northern Ireland lasted approximately eight months and was generally a very satisfactory experience. The spirit of camaraderie grew stronger as we learned to adjust to army life in a part of the United Kingdom which had strong economic and cultural ties with the port of Liverpool and its hinterland. I vividly remember one celebratory evening in particular in a public house in Strabane. A group of about fifteen of us went there to mark the birthday of Dougy Tabbard one of our most popular motor transport fitters. For the first time ever I rather foolishly mixed my alcoholic beverages with devastating effect. Then we headed en masse to the dance in the village hall sited on the opposite side of the road to our hostelry. My experience might be compared to 'feeling the swell' on a transoceanic crossing. I looked to the moon and it appeared to wobble as my legs behaved in a similar fashion. By the time we reached the dance floor I felt unable to join the more sober of my colleagues and was thankful to sit on the floor and spectate. When the end of the dance came we just managed to stagger out and catch the 'liberty' truck back to our billets at Newtown Stewart. My head was so sore the following morning that I vowed never to touch another drop of alcohol.

This training period kept me away from some of the heaviest bombing raids of the war in May 1941. These occurred during the Blitzkrieg of the Liverpool, Bootle, Birkenhead and Wallasey dockyards and many of their nearby towns on the banks of the River Mersey. It was a period of the Second World War when the enemy made its most desperate attempt to ruin the Port of Liverpool. It was believed that if the destruction of the dock system itself had been achieved then the moral of Merseyside would have been broken. These particular raids were to continue unabated for the first eight nights of the month and no other provincial city had to endure a cumulative attack of such magnitude. The attack on the night of 7th was unforgettable. I was informed by my family that about 300 extensive incidents had occurred within the boroughs of Liverpool and Bootle. Serious fires in both the dock areas and in the Liverpool City Centre caused devastation. They further informed me that there had inevitably been many grim scenes both inside and outside the docks. It was a major part of the Battle of the Atlantic and the defensive achievements of the Merseysiders and those who came from afar to help them was a crucial factor in winning the eventual victory against the enemy. It was some fifty years later – as I attended the Battle of the Atlantic Commemoration in

Liverpool – that the significance of such efforts were fully appreciated.

We, meanwhile, remained in Northern Ireland until Christmas time in that unforgettable year. Then news was received that the Division would have to return to England. We left the Irish shores and returned via the route we had entered the island, crossing the Irish Sea to Stranraer. It was a strenuous journey I remember, with the wartime hazards accompanied by those of severe frost on the dangerous roads. Having passed through Carlisle we journeyed over Shap Fell and stopped overnight, we were told, at Preston's Football Ground. We were unable to gain any worthwhile view of that historic stadium in the blackout conditions of war time.

On the next day, 23rd January 1942, we continued south until we reached Hayes in South London and then went on to West Wickham in Kent. Here we were billeted in a government commandeered semi-detached house. As we entered the house, which contained about six rooms I could not help my thoughts straying back to my family in Liverpool.

Outside Heyes Kent billet

Almost prophetically a few weeks later we were given embarkation leave. We were so pleased to accept this welcome break that we failed to consider the significance of this event. It was in fact to be the last time for four years that we would be able to enjoy the opportunity to be with our families and neighbourhood friends.

Almost ominously for me I returned to witness the near catastrophic effect that the heavy bombing raids had made on Liverpool. When I returned to West Wickham the next six to

H.M. King George VI Inspection at Oakley Park

Some of the lads of L.A.D. Group Heyes Kent

seven weeks were spent preparing for a somewhat mysterious long sea voyage to the Tropics. There could be no mistaking this, we agreed, when we were all issued with army tropical kit. Ironically, on 9th March, we prepared our vehicles for their journey to Liverpool for it was destined to be their port of departure. Three days later, before our turn to leave, we assembled in Oakley Park, near Hayes in Kent, for an inspection by King George V1. Three regiments in all – the Ninth, the Ninety First and the Ninety Second awaited his Majesty. He did indeed stop to make a few personal observations near me but unfortunately I did not hear his exact comments.

One week later, on 15th, we had one day's leave and this enabled me to photograph a small group of comrades from the L.A.D. at the rear of our billet in Wickham. Later I accompanied a friend, Fred Thurgood, to his home near Stanmore in North London for a weekend's leave. On my return I missed the last train for Hayes and had to sleep all night on a bench in Waterloo Station. This was to be the final chance I had to enjoy leave in England and the last opportunity I had to sleep in comfortable civilian bed for four years. On return the next morning we were lined up for 'vaccination' – protective inoculations against Typhus and Tetanus etc.

Chapter Two

Leaving for the Unknown, 1942.

Although I had lived most of my life in the seaport of Liverpool I had never sailed beyond the estuary of the River Mersey until 1942, when I was 27 years old. I had heard many exciting tales of the exotic 'ports of call' that my father had journeyed to in his travels as a merchant seaman. To me, until this time, however, such places had only been experienced in my imagination. The reality and indeed the accompanying dangers were now to be brought home to me in all their starkness.

On 19th March my comrades-in-arms and I finally left Hayes and were transported to Gourock, our Scottish port of departure. Soon after boarding that grand old ship of the sea, the 19,000 ton, S.S. Windsor Castle, we were aghast at the cramped space we had

Windsor Castle originally (Arundel Castle)

to settle into below the deck. The bedding which consisted, or so it seemed, of 'swinging hammocks' meant we felt like and happily christened ourselves as the 'ever-swinging troopers'. Even the prospect of a Waterloo railway station bench now seemed a more pleasant form for sleeping on.

Four days after our journey from Hayes we sailed from Scotland at 7am in the dim early morning light on 23rd March. Our ship formed but one vessel in a most impressive convoy. As the largest convoy of its type up to that point in the war we were to be given the protection of a flotilla of armed ships. These included the Aircraft Carrier Illustrious, later fated to be hit by a 1000lb. bomb in the Mediterranean Sea, the battleship Malaya, the cruiser Devonshire and a series of destroyers and corvettes. As we sailed forth on our historic voyage down the River Clyde we succumbed to an almost spontaneous outburst of 'community' style singing. The familiar, well-tried and often sentimental songs were lustily sang as many turned to grasp what was to be their last view of the British Isles. Many amongst us were never to return. With the hills of the North slowly receding to the strains of our melodic outburst we eventually gave way to the orders that complete silence was regarded as necessary to avoid detection by any enemy shipping.

One week later our ships were joined by a host of others and these, coincidentally, were from my native port of Liverpool. These included the warship Ramilles and the aircraft carrier Indomitable and a series of great ocean liners, i.e. the Duchess of Athol, the Almayora and the Franconia. As fate continued to spin its unforeseen web my brother, it later emerged, was at that time a merchant seaman aboard the latter merchant vessel. Another vessel of note was the Sobieski, a Polish ship which like the rest flew a barrage balloon above it to help frustrate air attack from any low flying aircraft. Each ship, too, also had its share of manned anti-aircraft guns.

Our most important means of defence, however, was firstly the screen of destroyers that continually wove a different pattern around us in the attempt to frustrate any would be U-boat attack.

Author on board 'Windsor Castle'

8 May 1942

Secondly our ship's course was a zig zag one that was employed sucessfully as we sailed towards the South Atlantic Ocean. Fortunately these dangerous manoeuvres were helped by the weather which remained particularly fine for this season of the year. Morale, fortunately, remained high as we, the troops, had ship's concerts, popular radio programmes and everyday games, such as Crown and Anchor, arranged for us on a regular basis. There were of course times of almost unbearable tension as, for example, when life-boat drills were undertaken. On an alert being sounded we had to scamper our way to pre-arranged points on the vessel's upper decks whereon we put on our life jacket and awaited any further essential instructions.

Having successfully negotiated the dangers of the North Atlantic we continued south to take one of the most historic of ancient trade routes to Freetown. This was infamously known as the White Man's Grave. Ironically it was to be our refuge for two days as the convoy vessels refuelled there for the next stage of its danger ridden mission. For two days, 5th to the 7th of April 1942, which it took to refuel the ships we were not allowed any shore leave whatsoever. Our only contact with the freedom of local civilian life was to watch with amusement as local native boys dived into the harbour to swim for any object the troops cared to throw overboard to them.

When we finally sailed on to the centuries old trading route to Durban via Cape Horn at the tip of the African continent we enjoyed some traditional fun. As we journeyed through the tropics and crossed the Equator we had the conventional 'Crossing of the Line' ceremony complete with a King Neptune and his ducking revels. To our lasting surprise we were greeted most hospitably by a multitude of generous citizens when we arrived in Durban, on 22nd April. They were remarkably kind to the troops of differing ranks and many of us were invited into their homes for meals and light entertainment. The home I was fortunate to be taken to was a beautifully furnished bungalow. Here I was encouraged to make apt use of the owners grand piano. As the family and several of my comrades gathered around it I played a host of war time favourite tunes, such as 'Take us Back to Dear Old Blighty', and was accompanied by lusty singing of the heartiest manner. They also took us to a film show to see Deanna Durban and Charles Laughton in 'It started with Eve'. We especially welcomed the ice cold drinks that they served us during the interval. We were all so touched by the generosity that we were pleased to accept the many invitations to give our names and addresses so that our hosts could write home to our families with the news of our well-being.

At the time of our enjoyment some of our former associates were engaged in action against the enemy. We later learned, for example, that the Thirteenth and Seventeenth Infantry Brigades went to prevent any likely invasion of Madagascar by the Japanese forces. The reality of this threat was brought home to us by one incident whereby a Japanese two-man submarine had penetrated beneath the vast numbers of vessels in Durban harbour and caused several casualties. H.M.S. Ramilles most notably began to list markedly after a foray by the submariners. Eventually the pair of predators left their craft and made their way to shore. They were noticeably shaken when their expectations of rescue by one of their own navy's seaplanes were dashed. They were promptly captured by allied commandos and held prisoners.

Shortly after this incident the Thirteenth and Seventeenth Infantry Brigades were relieved of their East African role by a Brigade of the King's African Rifles. The two former Brigades thereon were transported to the port of Bombay in the Indian sub-continent to join up with the Fifteenth there. One unfortunate consequence for the men of the Fifteenth was that many among their ranks were to suffer excessively from the twin attacks of malaria and sandfly fever.

Our own voyage to the sub-continent, we were informed, was

to take two weeks. On the day of our departure, 1st May, 1942, we heard that the Operations Commodore for India. had been transferred to our ship, the Windsor Castle, which was the Flagship of the expedition. Nine days out we again 'crossed the line' and duly noted how very warm it had become aboard our vessel. By night I was then able to sleep under one of the suspended lifeboats. A full-time lookout was kept for would-be Japanese raiders who were known to be operating throughout the Indian Ocean. We did experience one scare of note, when we heard an outburst of gunfire somewhere within our convoy. When no incident could be seen we believed, with relief, that any would-be attackers had been frightened off.

Through a dense heat haze, on 15th May, we were able to sight in the distance the Gateway to India. One day later when we

Author (left of picture)
in Bombay India

finally arrived at Bombay we were ordered to disembark and with rifles at the ready we marched through the streets of the port to be greeted by crowds of flag waving and cheering locals. Soon after we had arrived at the Colabar Camp we received instructions that we had been divided into two large units. Our unit based at the Camp was to be formed into road parties. The second had been assembled to prepare for a long rail journey.

The magnitude of our task did not come home to us initially because unknown to most of us an army division had never before crossed India by road. Our vehicles had not been designed to cope with the searing heat of the tropics, neither had we! Whereas some modifications could and were made to the vehicles we had to make our own 'adjustments' wherever possible to the frightening demands that were to be made on us. Our principal pre-occupation began with the need to protect the canvas water bottles that we were issued with. The rationed drinking water carried in them became a currency that was to assume a greater value than gold.

On the third day after our arrival we seized the opportunity during one-half day of leave to bathe on a shore lined with poplar trees. Known affectionately to us as Palm Beach it became the short-stay centre for large scale, gregarious male swimming and the playing of card games.

Palm Beach Bombay

In the evenings most of us went to the garrison's cinema before 'turning in' to sleep in tents which were characteristically surrounded by small walls of bricks to help reduce the menace posed by a host of insects. We had therefore had to adapt very rapidly to ward off a whole series of new dangers. These included the need to sleep inside mosquito nets and being on the lookout for the deadly small snake, the Kraite, which had the penchant of

Colarba Camp, Bombay, India. May 1942

crawling into any soldiers empty boots it might find. Avoiding alcohol in the noonday sun was an absolute must for each soldier as also was the need to cover our heads during the long daily hours of sunlight. We all had to consume as much suitable liquid as possible too. Any lapse in the numerous precautions such as those mentioned above often carried a deadly penalty. The failure to use a mosquito net correctly, for example, could lead after a bite to rough spasms of fever and endless cold sweats of soaking perspiration for the negligent. In a very short space of time therefore we had moved quickly into the incredibly debilitating life of a new-comer to the British Empire's tropical domains. I could not help but reminisce about those former but faraway freedoms of life in my native seaport of Liverpool. During several moments of nostalgia I would whimsically bring into my mind the wish that I could be back home "in Liverpool, in Liverpool Town where I was born". These were some of the words of a popular ballad. Its refrain concluded with the sentiment "there ain't no trees, nor scented breeze but the Black and Tan's flow free. It's six in a bed by the old Pierhead and it's Liverpool Town for me". Oh how wonderful, I thought it would have been to be able to spend just a few moments with the breezes of the River Mersey on my face and to have a strong pint of beer, or a 'Black and Tan' as I knew it, in my hand. Now the instructions 'Keep your mouth shut and your bowels open', from our beloved sergeant-major seemed the most important maxim for most of us in Bombay. As one comrade said "Bowels? I wasn't issued with them".

Chapter Three

Across India, 1942.

On 25th May 1942 our vehicles were finally unloaded from our ship in Bombay and we then drove to the military camp car-park for routine maintenance. Here we also carried out any essential preparation of them for their long 1,200 mile overland journey to Ranchi, a small town in the native state of Bihar, some eighty miles west of Calcutta. During our work period, preparing our vehicles for the long road journey which lay ahead of us, the intense heat of the day pressurised us to make numerous trips to the refreshment kiosk on the opposite side of the camp. Here we obtained ice cold drinks and ice cream but the latter melted before we arrived back. No sooner had we returned to continue with our work load, we found ourselves hankering to return to the kiosk for a repeat performance. I suggested laying a long tube between the kiosk and workshop to act as our continuous thirst quencher, or "Drink whilst you work".

Each vehicle was supplied with two chaghals, or large canvas

Road and Rail scenes Bombay

water bottles, and various additional petrol cans each containing four gallons of fuel in total. We did not have to wait very long before our momentous journey began. On the 8th June we left the Colabar Camp, in Bombay, about 6am. I was to co-drive a six-wheel stores lorry that was to experience only a few minor 'breakdowns' in 120 miles. We eventually arrived in Nasik, a very holy city, in the afternoon. After a well-deserved stopover we finally left there at 7.30am. the following day.

We suffered a series of problems at this stage, including grit both in the engines and the carburettors. Our first casualty came with the collapse of one of our colleagues who fell as a victim of the intense heat. So severe was the latter that the unfortunate soldier had to be evacuated by ambulance. Our relatively slow passage owed much to the many pot-holes pitted in the rough tracks of roadways. In turn many metal leaf springs in our vehicles suspension systems snapped and they had to be replaced more or less immediately. Our pace seemed to match that of one notable funeral procession that passed us at one of our enforced halts. To our amazement the uncovered corpse of the deceased, complete with painted red face and painted green feet, was propped in a sitting position in a chair held aloft by several bearers. Our slow progress was further curtailed by the innumerable obstructive bullock-carts. The drivers of the latter invariably directed their animals to move unpredictably to one side or the other of the rough cart-tracks. Much to our relief we arrived on the outskirts of Khaleitat to camp there in a huge field after travelling a total of 128 miles. The village of Khaleitat itself had some buildings of architectural merit but we generally classified them at this time as 'unfinished'. Not far from our camp, at the side of the main road, were many huts with their straw roofs and dried mud walls. In comparison with our conditions of life at home we agreed they lacked much in basic hygiene. Remarkably, fresh water for drinking for the local people depended on the ancient system of drawing it by the use of a tethered donkey that walked, above ground, around the well to draw up the priceless liquid.

By this point we fully accepted, with great reluctance, that it would be some time, if at all, before we returned to our now cherished way of life back home. An entirely different way of life, hitherto only known to us by way of school textbooks, or radio travel programmes, now unfolded for us. When we left Khaleitat, at 6.40am., 10th June, we dryly noted some local women undertaking their ritual washing on the river banks near their local temple. How distant and somewhat colder seemed our River Mersey in what would have been early summer back home. Here, in India, the turtles and crocodiles startled more than one local cart-driver. When we did eventually arrive in the next state, in India, we were warned about the dangers of the predatory, man-eating tigers in the State of Dhow.

Following a further exhausting journey of 110 miles we arrived at Mhow. On the following day, 11th June, we left to travel into ever increasing temperatures as our petrol fuel evaporated with worrying consequences. As our sturdy vehicles climbed into the hilly region the anxiety of a sudden engine stall was ever present. Though we took regular turns at steering our vehicle we tried everything in an attempt to reduce the personal debilitation caused by consistent intense perspiration. We opened the vehicle windows but the warmth of the hot breezes caused us to close them again. Our feet began to burn on the pedal controls even though we were wearing regulation sandals.

This enervating stage of our journey covered a relatively small stretch of some eighty five miles but we gratefully accepted the opportunity to stop in Biaora. On leaving, a day later, our stomachs turned with the sickly odours and stenches that stemmed from what appeared to us as prehistoric-like villages. Here the earth looked scorched and strewn with only dried up trees to shelter the inhabitants of the many mud huts. By the time we reached Shivpuri on this stage we had travelled 131 miles.

The thirteenth day of June became unlucky for us. We left Shivpuri on this day to drive into temperatures averaging 130.F. Few if any of us had ever travelled in such hellish heat before. More rough roads brought more broken suspension springs. The necessity to stop with each incident emphasised the unremitting, near helplessness of us as individuals. We had to face the extremes together and were dependent on our collective ability to pull through it if we were to survive. To our relief, after travelling through the Hades-like inferno we thankfully arrived in Jhansi, after some 136 miles travel. The Alexandra Barracks was our only stopping point for several days. The facilities, nonetheless, especially the canteen and cinema there, offered a welcome relief after the numerous discomforts of being 'on the road of hell-fire' that had exhausted us.

Fortunately, the two days following the unlucky thirteenth were more tolerable. They also turned out to be memorable. One of our colleagues, a signal driver, mistakenly swallowed some sulphuric acid in his haste to quench his thirst. That he appeared little worse for his actions seemed to speak volumes for the way our bodies were now accustomed to coping with the depredations of army life in the sub-tropics. When on one occasion we also saw a host of vultures picking at the remains of a water buffalo it aptly seemed to symbolise the fatality for any living creature that was deprived of its water supply for only a short period in this part of the earth. When news filtered through about the deluge of rain falling in Calcutta we longed for just a few moments in a shower of rain so common 'back home'. A stark contrast struck us too when, amidst all the relative poverty of life and resources around us, we passed one of the ruby and emerald studded doors of a local temple. When we also saw a sacred cow being allowed inside this place of worship and the utter poverty of most of the nearby inhabitants it only served to bring home to

First sight of elephants, relaxing for tea breaks Bombay area

us how much we were in a country of almost unparalleled extremes.

It came as no surprise when we left Jhansi by way of an army pontoon bridge that we heard our doctors were very busy treating cases of exhaustion. In all it was known that some thirty men in our ranks were very ill indeed. We also heard, with little surprise, that two members of the convoy ahead of us had died and were buried in Benares.

After a further enervating journey of 148 miles we arrived in Cawnpore, a town of some infamy during the Indian Mutiny in Queen Victoria's reign. We left the following day, 17th, and were upset but hardly surprised when we eventually heard that one of our officers died en route to Allahabad. With the temperature at our next main stop, in Aurangabad, rising to an unbearable 120º.F. in the shade and humidity nearing 95% we each had to face the stark reality of the question "who might be next?".

When we left Allahabad, after a stop-over of two days, we soon heard the answer to the former sinister question. As we crossed the great River Ganges, by way of a railway bridge, reports came through that a total of three soldiers had died. When we eventually passed through Benares we each began to realise how vulnerable we were too. In this, the hottest place we ever experienced, the temperature rose to a colossal 138º.F. The mood

The Ganges river bridge

among the men was a singular one of increasing concern. Would we see the day out? Were we going to die in this hellish heat without ever engaging the enemy in warfare?

When one of our drivers, at the steering wheel of a 15 cwt. truck, collapsed with heat exhaustion, our recovery vehicle went to his assistance. With every slight movement of their bodies causing them the greatest of discomfort, the recovery crew managed, after Herculean exertions, to use a crane to lift the vehicle so it could be taken on tow. During this event I rather foolishly went to investigate and to see if I could help in any way. Shortly after leaving the shade of my truck I suddenly began to feel uneasily queer. Fearing the worst, as my heart beat throbbed irregularly, I managed to force myself into an 'about face' position and returned slowly but awkwardly to the stores lorry. When I finally sat on the bed at the rear of the wagon, perspiring relentlessly, I again was suddenly confronted with the overwhelming feeling that "this is it, it's my turn now; how soon will it be?". Fortunately, and after a long period of anxiety, the suppressive thoughts and feelings of death passed from me. I recovered but to this very day have never known how the lads from the recovery wagon had driven in such totally strength sapping conditions.

The remaining days of that month in June in 1942 continued to be filled with events that if not, individually spectacular, were certainly dramatic. On the 18th we completed our ninety mile drive and finally arrived at Aurangabad thankfully at 6pm. The following day we left there in a slow moving convoy to travel the one hundred and eighty miles to Hazabagh. With the words of Noel Coward mockingly ringing in our ears we fully appreciated his prophetic words that only "mad dogs and Englishmen go out in the Mid-day sun". An Infantry Sergeant died at this point – another victim of heat exhaustion.

It came as no surprise, the very next day, that on our one hundred and seven mile trek to Hazaribagh the water-wagon was extremely over-worked. This was to be the last leg of this particular stage in our expedition across India. When we reached

Grub up at Ranchi   *Cinema at Ranchi*

our destination of Ranchi on 20th June we had crossed some 1,583 miles of the Indian sub-continent beyond Bombay.

Our camp was sited at a clearing in some woods outside the town. When we arrived it was uplifting to see that a cook-house was being erected as a priority. Food and drink, understandably, played a vital part in our tenuous hold over our everyday life. Two days after our arrival a further casualty occurred. The unfortunate soldier on this occasion was one Lieutenant Edwards. The 'grim reaper' we now fully appreciated was no respecter of rank.

One of a series of precautions we daily undertook in an effort to cling onto life was to queue for salt and fresh water to drink to help replenish the constant loss of body fluid through excessive perspiration. Other essential acclimatisation included the need to grow used to the howling jackals at night and the constant chirping of the crickets. By day we had to be on guard against the countless vultures and hawks that would swoop to empty any plate of food left unattended for even the briefest of moments. This seemingly endless cycle of watchfulness was dramatically interrupted on 23rd June when the first day of the monsoon rains began. When the heavens opened we were inflicted with a relentless deluge of heavy rainfall. It immediately brought a relief from the oppressive and excessive heat. At the same time, however, it caused the emergence of a most obnoxious stench which stemmed from the rottenness of the hitherto stagnant drains, ditches and sewers being disturbed.

Our daily chores such as the servicing of all our vehicles, was now made somewhat easier in the less 'clammy' atmosphere. Inevitably we had to provide innumerable replacements to those vehicles with damaged suspension springs. Fortunately, we were blessed with moments of welcome comic relief. On the 27th, for example, I was pleased to enter in my diary how our visit to the 'local cinema' in Ranchi village ended in mayhem. We went expecting the usual programme of a specially flown in U.S.A. film or an Indian film with sub-titles. During the performance a sudden commotion in one of the rows of seats was caused by the exclamation that "there's a tarantula spider beneath your seat". This was a shout clearly heard by most of the audience. In all my days as a film-buff - and this included cinema performances during the bomb alerts in Liverpool - I had never seen a cinema evacuated so quickly.

In time we actually became somewhat accustomed to the habits and habitat of the animal life of the region. Some of our favourite pastimes included the organisation of contests between centipedes or scorpions. Contrary to popular belief, as well we found, some snakes would crawl beneath our bedding mosquito nets and stay next to us harmlessly. In general they made no attempt to attack unless first attacked themselves. On other occasions our night-time dreams might be suddenly shattered through the efforts of other more minuscule creatures. Just like some scene from the Laurel and Hardy films we discovered that our wooden bed posts would often form a mysterious crust at floor level.

Scorpion

Without warning and often in the dead of night a bed would collapse with an accompanying explosive earthquake-like sound as the masses of red ants within the base of the bed posts finally devoured the base totally.

Such incidents help to relieve the tension that arose from time to time with news about the threatened assaults by the Japanese Army. The role of the Fifth Division was principally to repel any such invasion via either the north-east coastline of India or through the Jungles of Assam. In particular the Fifth was to defend the invaluable steel-works in Jamshedpur.

When it was apparent that the threatened Japanese Invasion of India had diminished significantly, a decision was made to transfer Reserve Divisions, such as the Fifth, to the European war front against Germany. With the Führer's forces threatening to break through in the Caucasus Mountains an ambitious plan was hastily drawn up in an attempt to prevent it. The uniqueness of the decision to move the Fifth lay in the fact that it would necessarily have to move over land by road, to the port of Basra, Iraq. The proposed route via the north-west Frontier, the Baluchistan Desert and thence from the South into the heartland's of ancient Persia was one with many inherent complexities. Part of the plan included the transporting of a second party of troops by rail.

As brief details of the plans to travel into the projected desert approaches filtered through to us there was a whiff of excitement experienced within all the units concerned. The feeding of the troops and the re-fuelling of their means of transport was extremely intricate as will be indicated below. With the assistance of the Indian military staffs these problems were eventually resolved. However, as we set out on this historic trek in torrential rain, 9th August 1942, the odds for success seemed completely stacked against us.

Chapter Four

From the Persian Gulf to Iraq, 1942-43.

Our departure from Ranchi, India on the 9th August, was delayed for about half a day because the roads had become flooded by heavy rainfall. This was something we were unaccustomed to back home even in the worst of British Summers! Nor were we used to the tribal disturbances which we heard might be a significant threat to our safety. It was because of this uncertainty that we were ordered to keep our revolvers 'at the ready'.

When our convoy made its way through Benares we experienced a rough ride that once more caused many broken suspension springs. These omnipresent pot-holes en route caused us even more broken springs as we went through Cawnpore and Pewar and then on to Agra.

A day stop, the 18th August, after a necessary slight diversion, enabled us to visit one of the 'wonders of the world', the Taj Mahal. We could not escape from making a contrast between this magnificent architectural monument and the abject poverty we had witnessed near Ranchi. Nor could we believe our good fortune when we were permitted to enter through the unique portals of that wonderful edifice. Before we were permitted to enter the sacred shrine we had to take off our heavy army boots and use the special slippers provided for us. I noted in my diary that the inlaid jewels in the exterior marble facia were 'just out of this world'.

The following day we were brought back to the reality of contemporary India as we pressed onwards on our journey. Moving slowly through Biaora, Mhow, Dulia and Masol we arrived at Bombay, 26th. August. At this juncture all our vehicles were taken on board a series of vessels that sailed ahead of us as an advance party.

On board SS Varella, Persian Gulf

Our turn to sail to Persia eventually came on 5th. September as we boarded a merchant vessel, the S.S. Varella. This had been converted from its use as a commercial vessel to act as a wartime troop-carrier. It was a relatively small craft that was easily tossed and turned as we headed towards the Persian Gulf. Our voyage lasted just over eight days but was sufficiently wild for almost all the troops, myself included, to be violently seasick.

Fortunately by 9th. September, 1942, as our convoy steamed up the Gulf waters, the sea became calmer. In a thick fog on the 13th. we anchored in the Bay and a religious service of thanksgiving was held on board. We remained on board in fact all the next day. One change in our routine was the freedom to watch the Arab 'date and tropical fruit walla', a ship-transported vendor, who pulled alongside our ship to conduct his business.

About six o'clock in the morning of the 15th September we 'weighed anchor' and sailed until; 10am. the following day when we arrived at Basra, reputedly also the home of the legendary Sinbad the Sailor. Once again it was back to basics as we undertook the necessary general duties and maintenance required in preparation for our next journey by road. Each vital mechanical part of our vehicles had to be checked. My job, for example, was to check the ignition systems. I cleared any sand from the distributors, the dynamos and the regulators. If any of the carbon brushes on the starter motors were worn, or covered with carbon dust, it was my responsibility to give them appropriate treatment. A faulty or inoperative starter motor would have meant that a vehicle could not be started and might cause unnecessary loss of vital time.

The need to be vigilant with our maintenance was soon brought home to us. When we left Basra, on 19th. September, we were confronted by vast sandy wastes with relatively poor tracks of roads, for mile after mile. The glare from the sun as it reflected on the sand was so dangerous to eyes that we were each issued with sun glasses with green tinted lenses.

This terrain, fortunately, gave way the following day to more wooded countryside that tended to suggest there was some underlying water table. When we had passed through several small towns we finally arrived at our first staging post and overnight stop. When we halted about 11pm. we learnt that it was called Khanjadwal and we had reached Mesopotamia. To our surprise we also discovered that Gurkha soldiers were in the camp. They were specially chosen to protect our lines of communication from any local tribal threats.

As we had arrived very late, owing to the considerable number of stoppages caused by mechanical or electrical failures, we were unusually hungry when we reached the camp. On this occasion our provisions of bully-beef and 'hard tack' seemed like a feast fit for a king. For once our dispatch rider, who brought the rations from our central stores, was a very popular figure.

Having heard of and read about how fabulous the ancient sacred city of Baghdad was we were, to our surprise, not unduly impressed by it. On 21st. September, as we passed through the eastern side of the city, the medieval style of most buildings looked only 'half complete'. Our destination within its

Two typical scenes of Baghdad

boundaries was the Lancer Camp site. Here we again carried out our routine maintenance and repairs of our vehicles.

In the evening a number of colleagues and myself were allowed 'leave' to visit this famous city of fine mosques, magic carpets and legendary thieves. Our meal in a small cafe was something of a disaster with the food quickly 'drying up', the peas were so hard we ended up playing ollies, or marbles, with them and the wine was excessively expensive. We were not unduly upset to leave the city with our convoy the following day. Having travelled some 358 miles from Basra to Baghdad we had grown accustomed to driving across rough terrain. Now, as we headed east and made our way towards ancient Persia the fresh greenness of our own homeland seemed a distant but cherished memory.

We were informed that our new destination lay in the Caucasus, north of Tehran. Here it was believed our enemy, the German army, or 'Gerry'. was threatening to make a breakthrough. En route we arrived at Khaniquin City in the north to encounter mile after mile of Polish refugee camps. After an overnight stop we left the city confines to drive up through the terrifying Paitak Pass.

The terror of this journey for us lay in the confrontations we had with the drivers of the African convoy troops taking personnel parties up to Persia. The drivers of these vehicles drove as though possessed by demons. They had little fear of the steep ravines that stretched below the barrierless rough mountain tracks that our vehicles had to surmount. Some drivers, it was widely believed, had 'shot off' the roads and plummeted hundreds of feet below.

Thankfully we reached the garrison town of Kermanshah on the 28th. Here we stopped at the the nearby camp that was at the foot of the tall, rugged mountains of Taqui Bustan. The whole division was renunited by the 5th October 1942. We later discovered that some six miles north of Kermanshah was a well which was reputed to have been discovered by Moses in Biblical times. Our stop, which lasted several weeks, was some 701 miles from Basra. It was to be one of our longest stays in this part of the world. This stoppage enabled us to prepare thoroughly for our next 'stiff climb', through the Shah Pass.

The stop-over also gave us the opportunity to rest and take stock of our lives. We were able to reflect on the general progress we had made in the war and we were able to think back about those times of normality we had enjoyed as civilians. Our free time was often to be thoroughly enjoyed thanks to the efforts of the Entertainment's and National Service Artists, more famously known as ENSA. Our meals, too, which included sausage, mashed potatoes, dried meat, vegetables and tinned fruit puddings, was remarkably tolerable under such conditions. I felt therefore when I underwent a tooth extraction at the camp that I should not blame Bill Wignall, our cook!

Nor were we forgotten in this seemingly distant outpost of the war by the upper echelons of the armed services. Lord Trenchard, the Marshall of the Royal Air Force, for example, visited us on 30th. October, 1942. Shortly after his visit a newly formed unit, the Royal Electrical and Mechanical Engineers, was constituted and my colleagues and I, in the L.A.D. were transferred to it. In keeping with military discipline all units, including ours, were amassed to attend the Commemorative Armistice Service of World War One, on Sunday 8th. November.

It was brought home to us that within the previous three months, the Fifth Division had twice crossed India and had moved into Iraq and Persia with relatively few casualties. This we knew at first hand had involved an extremely complex series of moves and its successful outcome was a source of subdued pride for the Divisional Commander, Major General Berney-Ficklin, C.B. M.C.

As a vital part of our preparations we purchased yellow, wool-lined, sheepskin poshteens. These were to combat the severe cold we were warned we would encounter in the next stage of our journey. On the Friday after our Service we moved

Climbing the Pytak and Shah Pass

out of Kermanshah. This time we were placed at the head of the procession of military vehicles. Our L.A.D. group lead the way with the Armament Sergeant Major and myself co-driving the Dodge Truck. Two Austin stores lorries and the Leyland recovery vehicle completed our unit.

Fortunately, though we occasionally had to stop for 'breakdown' incidents there was no major problem to confront. This was a blessing because it was becoming increasingly much colder. We even lost the main convoy after one of these breakdowns but eventually arrived - extremely cold and hungry - at an open camp which was sited away from the main road. As good fortune favoured us, we found a hot meal welcomingly awaiting us there.

After only a few hours sleep we left this camp at 7am. the next morning with the prospect of negotiating the Shah Pass. This fearful phenomenon was reputed to be the highest in the World. This, with gradients at a ratio of between 1 to 3 and 1 to 4, posed the most severe of operational tests. Attached to each of our store lorries, with their own substantial loads, were field guns. Our lorries crawled up these gradients at 'walking pace' in a demanding climb of about some 5,000 feet. Fortunately, the total excessive towing loads for each vehicle were helped in a small way by a special set of low gears on the stores lorries. The gears had to be operated by a lever between the two seats at the rear of each cab.

Our 'reward' for finally overcoming the excessive friction in such an operation was a pot of 'bully-stew'. This we collectively devoured when we arrived about 10.30pm. - in extremely cold conditions - at the camp at Hamadan. Such was the nervous energy loss in the exercise that we ate and re-filled our Billy Cans two or three times each. When we finally climbed into our cosy sleeping bags at the back of the stores lorries we did not need any rocking lorry to help us to fall asleep.

After this welcome rest we began the final part of our trek, on 16th. November. In the late evening of that day, at about 9.30pm., having crossed part of the Persian Plain we arrived at the Holy City of Qum. In this position, miles from civilisation and in extreme cold, we 'dug in'. It looked as though we were in for a very hard winter. As we reflected how much conditions had altered from our time in India we dug out earth to an approximate depth of three foot. These trenches were covered only by tents of unusually thick canvas. When we were also instructed to dig an adjacent rectangular trench, some twelve feet by four, to a depth of eight feet our inquisitiveness was quickly answered. This was to be our toilet 'facility'. Fortunately, our sense of humour helped us to overcome the unhygenic inconvenience. Since it failed to offer any heating for 'cold bums' we refused it a five star rating. More appropriately it was down-graded and renamed the 'News Centre'!

Our daytime general duties did help to keep us warm. In our off duty periods, too we organised demanding, physical games. Football and jogging competitions were the favourites, as they kept our temperatures high as long as possible. Our main view by daylight was dominated by the 18,549 feet high, snow-covered conical dome of Mount Dermavend. It was a general heartfelt wish, as we gazed in awe of this magnificent feature that dominated thousands of square miles of salt desert, that we never had to cross the arid plain in front of it. Those assigned to guard duty at night were each armed with a Smith and Wesson 0.38 revolver. Such was the intense night-time cold that two hour periods of duty were regarded as the limit of endurance.

One day in late November I joined a party of my comrades to take a liberty truck into Qum. Our shopping expedition into the market place was rather mundane and would probably have been a great anti-climax for Ketelbny the composer of the musical work In a Persian Market!

Following this leave from duty we returned to camp. The ensuing few weeks were memorable for their lack of freedom and the return to the more serious side of 'soldiering'. On 29th., for example we were on Bath Parade. We were rounded up and taken into Qum to use some specially constructed baths there. As we journeyed in we were told that some of the territory of the state of Turkey could be seen lying ahead of us. Afterwards we reflected how we would have preferred a warm Turkish bath to the cold one we had to use.

When we entered the month of December our thoughts inevitably strayed to the Christmas preparations back home. Meanwhile we were called upon, on 7th. of that month, to join a Divisional 'shoot'. This entailed us all joining in with the artillery practice on a special firing range. Before this encounter we were ordered to dig up part of one of the roads that passed beneath a railway bridge. This eventually allowed our high sided recovery wagons to negotiate the route under the bridge and speed up their crossing time of the railway route. When we finally reached the firing range, a somewhat desolate expanse of open land we stayed there overnight using our sleeping bags and drawing our water from a local well.

Just over a week later we left our camp in a different direction than on the previous occasion and after an eighteen mile journey had yet a further divisional shoot. Traversing very desolate terrain through a mountain pass we could not help but think of the three wise men and their epic journey over 'field and fountain, moor and mountain'! Unlike these famous travellers we returned to camp, extremely cold and hungry. Thankfully, our cook Bill Wignall, was able to rectify some of our discomfort. His hot-pot, or bully-stew with 'hard tack' biscuits seemed to us like a meal fit for a king.

After this feast on 25th. December he prepared a Christmas dinner, which seemed like a banquet to us. This included roast potatoes, beef, cabbage and Persian, not Yorkshire, puddings. These delicacies, like the Christmas pudding that followed, were served in traditional style by our officers. On Boxing Day we 'topped' off our celebrations by holding our own special L.A.D. dinner in our little 'mess'.

Even in this far flung and somewhat desolate spot ENSA did manage to reach us. On 29th. December the well-known comedian - later to become an international comic film star - Terry Thomas arrived with a programme called 'Your Welcome'.

These and other such 'shows' were a tremendous boost to the morale of my colleagues and myself. Our constant vigil in such far away places, seemingly miles from any shred of civilisation, led us often to believe that we were the forgotten men. The commonly used phrase the 'legion of the lost' regularly sprang to mind. When an artist like Terry Thomas did manage to reach us it brought a bright light of hope into our darkest hours of despair. Many other stars, such as George Formby, Vera Lynn, Marlene Deitrich and Gertrude Lawrence, trod the small primitive, portable stages in a similar fashion. Their treks into the many lonely landscapes in a variety of inclement weather conditions embodied a type of heroism that was unique in itself.

At a later date, after the War had ended, it was interesting to read the biographies of others, such as Harry Secombe and Spike Milligan, and hear of their experiences. From their side of the stage they described the need to perform on makeshift stages and their impromptu necessity to learn their craft quickly. For the troops in their audience, who might never see another show for several months at a time, the overriding spur for the 'stars' was to lift their morale to such a height that it would sustain them for a lengthy period of time. The most poignant and moving moments for such entertainers were usually experienced when they performed in the numerous makeshift hospital wards. There they had to confront the realisation that many of the critically wounded would most probably not see another show.

Camp site near Qum

Whilst such visitors helped to relieve the feelings of stagnation, isolation and frustration that often crept into our lives, our chief concern was to seek out any news of "when are we going home"? On New Years Day, 1943, the lads and myself in the L.A.D. did not have the resilience to 'let in' the New Year. So low were the overnight temperatures that our principal defence against heat loss was to lay in our sleeping bags with as many as eight huddled together. We then topped these huddled heaps with up to a dozen blankets. The only sign of life must have been those red noses that protruded from these mounds.

One soldier from our 'merry band' had bought an old hand-powered gramophone in one of the markets in Tehran. On the Ninth Day of Christmas, 2nd. January 1943, we spent most of the day listening to some scratched sounding 78 rpm records. The following day there was a small pox case reported in the camp and needles were used in these circumstances to have the entire camp vaccinated. A further set-back occurred on the 7th. January, when as a result of a tremendous cloud burst Bill Wignall's cookhouse caved in. What a disaster this was for instead of a regular cooked roast meal we had to eat cold bully beef sandwiches each day.

January and February in fact were to be the last two months that we spent as the 'forgotten men' in Persia. A succession of minor events was interspersed by two happenings of note in the direction of the War. I noted, for example, that on 9th. January after the Adjutants Inspection on what must have been on one of the most desolate 'parade grounds' in the World we undertook a recreational training session. The principal feature of the latter was a football match arranged by representatives from the officers and the lower ranks. A week later all leave to Tehran was postponed as a snow blizzard raged around the camp. The snow fell for more than three days. There were some lighter moments fortunately, such as another gramophone 'concert' in the recreation tent and a more formal concert organised for us in Qum. About this time, too, one of our fitters a Francis Tack, caused a near sensation. Affectionately known as 'Smell Franky' he mistakenly heated up paraffin, instead of water for washing himself. Many believed that he had in reality forgotten what water looked like!

On a more serious level we heard on 7th. January that Iraq had formally declared war against the Axis powers. Two weeks later news reached us that the incomparable defences mounted by the Russians at Stalingrad had caused a disaster for the German forces engaged on that front of the war. As a consequence the Allied sweep towards the Caucasus Mountains and into the Persian Plain, en route for the Middle East, put paid to the Gerry onslaught there. The highly trained British Fifth Division, with its vast experience in this region no longer needed to be kept in reserve in Persia and could be actively used elsewhere. The much awaited Mediterranean Offensive was already being planned in Cairo. The historic battle of El Alamein had been won by the Eighth Army and we were now set to join them.

Meanwhile our February activities mirrored those of January to a large degree. We underwent further inoculations - this time against typhus and dyptheria - with a Colonels inspection on the 7th. to emphasise the need for rigid hygiene precautions in a region infamously known for its extensive range of dangerous diseases. When Bill Wignall went into hospital for ill-health we largely had to fend for ourselves at meal times. Leave was granted for a three day visit to Tehran and a further football match - between Regimental Headquarters and L.A.D. was arranged.

On 28th February we began preparations to move onwards from the camp-site. When the Eighty Second Recovery Unit was assigned to join us, it was believed that numerous breakdowns must have been anticipated. Our high spirits in planning to move on from general almost intolerable conditions were dampened when adverse weather conditions in the Shah Pass caused the exodus to be postponed. By 1st. March, however, with special attention being given to brake checks on all vehicles and to the issue of wheel chains on tyres we realised that the route ahead was to be exceptionally hazardous.

Chapter Five

Preparing for the Mediterranean Offensive, '43.

By this time in our travels we began to have some insight into the deeds of the early great explorers in this part of the world. Though our progress was helped by the modernity of our vehicles compared to the reliance on beasts by the great travellers of the past, it was still dangerous, stressful and arduous for us.

We knew of course that the first obstacle we had to overcome was the 8,000 to 10,000 foot high Shah Pass. When we left our camp, on 2nd March, we did so in the depth of a cruel winter. Road journeys were particularly demanding with mile after mile

L.A.D. Group in front of Austin stores lorry

of fog, snow and ice to be faced. My role was again to be that of co-driver, with my colleague Bob Naylor, in an Austin stores vehicle. The incessantly cold temperatures, some as low as minus 28º.F, lead to carburettors and brakes freezing in many vehicles.

It was quite remarkable that there was so few serious accidents en route. After the first stage of some 84 miles we arrived at Sultanabad, about 7.30pm. in the evening. There was very little time to rest because on the following morning we had to be ready to leave promptly at 8am. During the day we heard of an accident in the mountainous terrain, a signal truck overturned and had to be rescued by our unit's Leyland recovery vehicle. Though this delayed our progress for some time none of the crew were reported to be fatally injured. They were only badly shocked most probably because of the slow speed, (between 5 and 15 mph.,) which we were forced to travel at. After a total of 74 miles we arrived at Malaya. Once again this was only an overnight stopping place and we left there at 9.30am on the 4th. Fortunately we were able to take advantage of a relatively sound, tarmacadamed road and after a day of no significant problems we reached Hamadan, about 56 miles away, at 6.40pm.

Our good fortune of the previous day changed when , on 5th March, we left Hamadan and descended through many dangerous steep bends. Some of the gradients over one particular seven mile stretch had a ratio of 1 in 3 or 1 in 4. The most unfortunate amongst us were probably the motor cycling Don Rs, who were regularly thrown from their machines after skidding on steep slopes. This must have been particularly hurtful to those whose hands were frozen to their handle-bars. Whereas the heavy vehicle drivers could have their hands massaged to improve the circulation as they drove, the motor cyclists had no such help. When we stopped, after some 66 miles, to sleep overnight in a field we felt matters could not get worse.

When we moved on at 8am. on the 6th March it was through moderately-sized hills. Nevertheless we did not escape from the severe cold and snow blizzards which persisted every inch of the way to Chehar Zebab Camp, our next destination, 25 miles south of Kermanshah. Though there were fewer mishaps than previously one of the recovery vehicles, towing a 3 ton truck which had broken down, did not arrive until 9.30pm.

Our next phase for a major descent was planned for our encounter with the Paitak Pass on the following day. We realised when we left the Chehar Zebab Camp that more dangerously steep bends and gradients lay ahead. Once again we descended for the most part in bottom gear and when some of the motor-cyclists brakes froze we had no option but to increase our own vehicles load by tying the bikes to the rear ends. When we finally reached the bottom of the Pass, some six miles long we made a temporary camp there.

When we did move on we welcomed the noticeably warmer air and the fact that we were able to reach some 30 to 40 mph. in our vehicles. Soon after we crossed the Iran-Iraq border we reached Kanaquin City in the mid-afternoon. There was some light relief the following day, as we left Kanaquin at 6am and headed for Baghdad. After about 12 miles travel from the signposts we had used we discovered that the posts must have been 'rotated' which sent us off in the wrong direction. We eventually arrived at the famous city at 5.00pm, after some 125 miles travel, to stay at the Lancer Camping Ground.

For the first time in several months we were allowed some leave. Having carried out our maintenance check duties I joined a party that went into the Rashid cinema. How we marvelled at the chance to see a first class film 'Son of Fury'. The internationally known stars of the film Tyrone Power, George Sanders, Roddy McDowall and Elsa Lancaster, provided us with many talking points after their sound performances. Fortunately, too, the news features were spoken in two languages, both Arabic and English, as they were screened on a special screen sited alongside the main screen. For a short time afterwards we were able to tour through the local shops. Before I caught a taxi back to camp, some 2.5 miles away I bought an ornate ring for 750 local fils.

Our chance to settle into some of the relatively civilised

facilities of Baghdad soon disappeared. By 11th March we were leaving the City to head for Syria via Transjordania. Though the 'tarmac' roads were much easier to use than some of the rougher ones mentioned earlier a new danger loomed ahead of us. Intense raging sandstorms that battered our vehicles had to be suffered. Nevertheless we were grateful for the warmer air curents after experiencing the terrifying cold of the previous mountain regions. When we arrived at Wadi Muhammadi after a journey of some 128 miles we were somewhat pleased to feel blood circulating through our veins once again.

The gypsy-like life we had become accustomed too continued again at 7am. on 12th when we left the desert camp at Wadi Muhammadi. Now we found that sand seemed to enter every nook and cranny of our vehicles. Our carburettors were especially affected by the problem. When we arrived at Rutbah, at sunset, for the first time in many months I felt relaxed enough to appreciate the beauty of a sunset in this distant land.

From time to time, we experienced some near comic incidents that we had seen our favourite film star comedy teams involved in. On the 13th March, just a few miles away from Rutbah which we left at 6.30 am, our recovery vehicle collided with a local orange-laden lorry. The Arab driven vehicle had been heading in the opposite direction to us and was left badly damaged with its colourful load scattered across the road. We never did find out what became of them. On this unlucky date, as we passed through the frontier, we followed a branching track from the main road that at first seemed to lead us nowhere.

A recovery truck before and after an accident

Three hours after leaving Rutbah we arrived at a pumping station known as H 4 where we rested until 4 o'clock in the afternoon. Although the road from here was very flat and soundly surfaced it was strewn with wisps of the camel thorn plant and many small round stones. Whilst neither of these caused any trouble, the sand in the carburettors and dynamo regulators of the motor-cycles caused great problems. As we stopped at Mafraq in Jordan the slight shades of green visible in the patchy grass adjacent to the route proved a welcome sight to us.

Once again, on leaving Mafraq in the early hours of 15th March, we encountered the dangers of rapid descent by road. Once more we had to tackle a steep winding road with a seemingly endless number of mind-numbing bends. Our 'reward' was that we eventually passed through the Palestine frontier and entered into what indeed seemed to us to be the Promised Land of Biblical renown. Here there was an abundance of greenery, with orchards and orange groves and many other types of fruit trees.

Our arrival at 6.30 at Wathaya Camp after a journey stage of 129 miles, permitted us to rest and carry out our customary vehicle maintenance. In general, morale was now quite high for in spite of the rigours of the journey most of the men regarded their experiences as a type of adventure that they had never expected to undertake at any point in their lives.

When we left at 7am we continued south through Gaza. Seeing a First World War British soldiers Cemetery there was a poignant reminder of the frailty and shortness of our lives. Having passed through Beersheba we moved along more soundly-surfaced tarmac roads through desert-like terrain. Finally, at sunset we arrived desparately hungry at a desert camp near Ismailia at the Suez Canal. The usual hot meal there of sausage and 'mash', with dehydrated potatoes an essential ingredient, was most satisfying.

At this stage in our trek we were informed that we were about to complete the last few final parts of our epic journey. From here on, unknown to us, the 'fine-tuning' of our Divisions preparations for the invasion of Sicily was to be undertaken. There was to be a great deal of Divisional training to rehearse, for example, the complicated process of getting troups to climb down into those landing craft some distance from the invasion beaches. A specialised series of large-scale boat drills for disembarkation were continuously practised. Our Division had thus entered the fitness routines that were to become so vital in our future fighting role from Syracuse to Rome. On 19th March we left Ismailia at 7am. Our next destination was to the west through more desert sandstorms. We reached Kabrit Camp, sited to the north of the Suez Canal System, at 1.0pm. Having now travelled a total of 1,765 miles by land we welcomed the three week stay there.

We immediately began the task of servicing and renovating our transport vehicles. It felt as though we removed half the sand in the desert terrain by the time we had cleaned them thoroughly. Under the watchful eye of Armament Sergeant Major Gilmow the L.A.D. men and myself were billeted in large marquees. This form of compulsory communal living made the privacy of life back home seem but a dream. Although we did enjoy the occasional trip to a local 'Yankee' . or American style cinema, we had to meticulously plot our return to camp by compass. The camp was some two or three miles away and there were no distinctive landmarks. There had been no such problem for Bing Crosby, Bob Hope and Dorothy Lamour in the humorous film 'Road to Singapore' which had been the main feature film we saw on one of our visits!

To say the visits to the cinema were a stable fillip to our lives at this time would be no understatement. On 28th March two days after a second visit to the cinema we had a further half-day leave in Ismailia. On this occasion we tried another venue, the King Farouk cinema, which was named in honour of the head of the Egyptian Royal Family.

As we entered the month of April our thoughts returned to the memories of Spring at home. On the 3rd of that month we visited the Shafto cinema for a special showing of 'Next of Kin'. Although it was something of a propaganda film, starring Melvyn Johns, Nova Philbeam and Basil Radford in the roles of a British war-time family, it was very entertaining and touched a sentimental note in reminding us of life 'back home'.

Such brief flirtations with the 'normality' of life in Britain were short-lived. The following day, for example, a severe sandstorm raged having come onto us from nowhere. Two of our giant tents collapsed with soldiers still in bed in the early morning. The men not surprisingly hardly knew what had hit them. When we were all invited, three days after this incident, to the local airport's American cinema, it was a major treat. Our American hosts, as was customary for them throughout the war, made us most welcome and provided us with refreshments. I particularly enjoyed some of their cans of beer and a chance to speak to two U.S.A. servicemen from Colorado and Rhode Island.

Author in jovial mood.

By the middle of the month, however, we were on the move again. On 11th April we left Gneifa to head towards Cairo. Some 8 miles to the north of this fabled Egyptian city we stopped, at Almaza Camp, near Heliopolis. By now we noted we had journeyed some 1,870 miles in total from Qum. One of our chief tasks here was to paint our vehicles in camouflage. This was the clearest indication so far that we were finally to become active combatants in one of the main theatres of the War. We thereon seized the opportunity for leave with perhaps more eagerness than hitherto. At 5pm. on the 12th April we hopped onto a tramcar and went into the city to tour the cafe's, bars and cinemas. Whenever possible we engaged in English conversation with the local inhabitants but learnt very little from them about the direction of the War.

The following week we returned to the city and dined at one of the roof garden cafe's. Later we went to the Opera House for

The Sphinx   *Pyramid and River Nile*

a variety show. The following day, 15th April 1943, we undertook our last trip into Cairo. Taking a bus ride we visited the world famous Pyramids and Sphinx. We were treated to a cabaret performance in the evening and felt that this might well be the 'lull before a storm'. Arriving back at camp at 1.30am we were resigned for the arduous nature of the journey we were about to embark on.

The next stage of our journey was through more territory that was well known throughout the civilised world for the part it played in Biblical Times. On 16th April we left the Heliopolis Camp, for the last time. We then took a route that was unknown to us alongside the Suez Canal. After covering some 95 miles we reached another army camp some 2 miles north of Ismalia. Over the next three days we travelled in excess of 200 miles. Our path led in us through Palestine, Gaza and then into the Jordan Valley. By the 19th of April we had reached the Sea of Galilee and on the following day reached the Lebanon frontier where we stayed overnight at a camp north of Qatana.

After this trek from Heliopolis we had covered a total of 567 miles. When we rested at our chosen camp, Qatana near Damascus, we were pleased to settle again in one place, if only for 17 days. In this case we were able to enjoy the unique feeling that we were living where some of the famous Biblical stories had been enacted. The atmosphere for a Christian believer as I was, was almost indescribable. A visit to Bethlehem and to the Chapel believed to be on the site of the manger used by the new born Jesus was particularly memorable.

Down town Beirut   *Damascus*

Having carried out our vehicle maintenance and other general duties we were also offered a chance, on the 7th May 1943, to visit Beirut. This trip was by far and away one of the nearest we came to enjoying the life of a holiday tourist. To start our adventure, which lasted three days, we left Damascus by train in mid-morning. Once we had been hauled up by a ratchet-powered system up a very steep mountain side we were eventually able to see Beirut in the distance. There we stayed at a seaside holiday camp, enjoying lunch-times at the 'Kit Cat Cafe'. Inevitably we indulged in our favourite past-time, a visit to the Empire cinema. Among the feature films I recall, was 'Spring Parade', made in 1940, with Deanna Durban in the singing role, together with the popular Robert Cummings and Mischa Auer. A more appropriate film, particularly for the 'gung ho' style attitude of our American allies was the movie 'The Shores of Tripoli'. For our part, with our first-hand war-time experience of the bombing of British cities, many amongst us knew it was unwise to over glamorise the course of the war in any form whatsoever.

Since all 'leave' passes were made out to 11.59 hours we usually stayed out, if near the holiday camp, till about 11.30pm. At long last, 9th May, we went for dinner at the Hotel Metropole. Following on from this many of us went on to the Y.M.C.A. for the much heralded community singing in the large lounge. We all lustily joined in to sing many of our favourite songs such as 'Bless 'Em All, A Long Way to Tipperary, When the Sergeant Major's on Parade and Lilly Marlene'. After this session we at last had some time to write home. As our good fortunes continued I noted that the following day was a beautiful one and enabled my colleagues and myself to walk along the seafront promenade. We had lunch at the Y.M.C.A. and in the evening we went on to the Grand Theatre to see the review 'Balalaika'.

My enjoyment did not cease immediately I left the holiday camp to return to military camp. After three marvellous days leave I and my friends left Beirut by train at 7.00am 11th May. We stopped at Ryak. half-way back for lunch at the NAFFI there. The hitherto leisurely normality of our routine maintenance and repairs duties was shattered with a bang as we were introduced to a new Armament Sergeant Major Sheriff.

Following a half-day's leave in Damascus, for shopping and an evening cabaret show, my good fortune began to wane. On 20th May a small infection, resulting from a hornet bite on the back of my hand, began to swell painfully. By 4pm. the following day, following a further night of agony because of my swollen wrist and hand, I had the sore lanced by the medical officer. Nor was I the only one afflicted because George Dalloway, a welder by army trade, returned from hospital on 25th May after a bout of malaria.

By the end of the month our time in the middle east was, thankfully in many ways drawing to a close. Preparations began in earnest for a venture that was to take us in a new direction. The first visible sign of this turn in events was when we left 'en masse' from Damascus at 7am. on 7th June to head, via Nazareth, for an assembly camp 8 miles from Haifa. We knew that a few days earlier two of our stores lorries and a recovery truck had also travelled to the seaport to board a ship. When we began the water-proofing routines for all our vehicles we realised that we were most probably preparing for an amphibious invasion of dramatic proportions.

Our suspicions were confirmed when we were ordered to drive our vehicles into another section of the camp for the scrutiny of special inspectors! The following day we drove each 'finished product' to the dock quayside to Shed Number One to await their boarding of a ship. It fell to A.S.M. Sheriff and myself to sleep on board one of the vessels to take guard duty watch from 2 to 4am. Once again the events of the ensuing days seemed to follow in quick succession. On 13th May we were taken to a transit camp about 1 mile north of Haifa. The next morning we went on parade at 8am., were taken onto the beach for physical training and then route marched for some 8 miles around the seaport. When we finally arrived at 'tea-time' we enjoyed the relaxation offered for the rest of that day in the Church of Scotland's canteen there.

After the next parade, the following morning we were informed that we would soon move on to a nearby monastery. It at once brought to my mind Ketelby's work 'In a Monastery Garden' .Fortunately, after yet a further route march on the beach on the next day we were led to St. Joseph's canteen, in Haifa, for our meals and allowed to visit the barracks cinema nearby. This came as a prelude to what proved a most upsetting anti-climax the next day.

Train leaving Beirut

When we marched to Haifa's railway station after our 8pm. parade on 17th, we saw that in one of the sidings was a lengthy goods train. As we waited patiently for about one hour we hopefully anticipated that we were waiting for a passenger train to arrive. There was no such good fortune because the officer in charge eventually bawled out "all aboard" and pointed to the 'cattle truck' style of wagons nearby. After climbing into them the train moved off quite rapidly. It came as no surprise when we all joined in the spontaneous singing of 'We're the Old Cow Hands from Blighty Land'.

Travelling through the night in this crude form of transport we eventually passed into Gaza and eagerly had breakfast, around

6am. on the 18th June, in the station canteen. Next it was on to Quatana for dinner at 4.30pm. and a trip through Ismalia to reach the Zagazz-Benha camp site about 3 hours later.

The next stage of our epic journey took us through Tanta, in Egypt, about 2.30pm and then on to Damahur-El-Amira, for 'breakfast' at 5 o'clock that morning in the railway station. Finally, once fed we no longer had to use our 'bone-shaker' cattle trucks but boarded motor vehicles instead. Our destination now was to be a camp near what was to become a symbol of our good fortune El-Alamein.

By now, little by little and at first hardly noticeable, there was a growing feeling of excitement in our daily lives. Our thoughts became more and more pre-occupied with the real prospect of front-line action. As we put up our tents, on 19th June 1943, we were a little 'down in the mouth'. This seemed more so after expectantly awaiting our mid-day meal; we were again dismayed by the presentation to us of 'hard tack', or bully beef and biscuits. "Was this to help us fast?" we mockingly asked before we went into action.

Our final ten days of June 1943 seemed to fly past at an ever increasing pace. On the 20th we had our church parade and it was led by a padre wearing the rank of Lieutenant Colonel. After this there was an unusual number of occasions to relax from the more humdrum general duties of army life. We had come to expect that such relaxation was often the prelude to a more dangerous period of anti-enemy action. We usually accepted any such opportunities, however, whenever they arose. On 21st I remember attending a delightful concert in the Royal Airforce Camp at El-Alemein. During each day we had further sessions of physical education that seemed to auger the need for fitness for the tests that lay ahead. By night the chance to visit the camp cinema – to see 'Tales of Manhattan' – I vividly remember at this time was gratefully accepted. What a treat it was to see such a splendid film. Based on the story of a tailcoat handed on from the owner to new owner it had a star-studded cast which included Charles Boyer, Rita Hayworth, Thomas Mitchell, Eugene

Paulette, Ginger Rogers, Henry Fonda, Roland Young and Edward G. Robinson. As was the custom we applauded with thunderous gusto at the conclusion of the performance.

Two evenings later there was an E.N.S.A concert which often seemed to occur, we later realised, before an event of major

General Montgomery

EIGHTH ARMY

PERSONAL MESSAGE FROM THE ARMY COMMANDER

To be read out to all Troops.

1. The time has now come to carry the war into Italy, and into the Continent or Europe. The Italian Overseas Empire has been exterminated; we will now deal with the home country.

2. To the Eighth Army has been given the great honour of representing the British Empire in the Allied Force which is now to carry out this task. On our left will be our American Allies. Together we will set about the Italians in their own country in no uncertain way; they came into this war to suit themselves, and they must now take the consequences; they asked for it, and they will now get it.

3. On behalf of us all, I want to give a very hearty welcome to the Canadian troops that are now joining the Eighth Army. I know well the fighting men of Canada; they are magnificent soldiers, and the long and careful training they have received in England will now be put to very good use—to the great benefit of the Eighth Army.

4. The task in front of us is not easy. But it is not so difficult as many we have had in the past, and have overcome successfully. In all our operations we have always had the close and intimate support of the Royal Navy and the R.A.F., and because of that support we have always succeeded. In this operation the combined effort of the three Fighting Services is being applied in tremendous strength, and nothing will be able to stand against it. The three of us together —Navy, Army and Air Force—will see the thing through. I want all of you, my soldiers, to know that I have complete confidence in the successful outcome of this operation.

5. Therefore, with faith in God and with enthusiasm for our cause and for the day of battle, let us all enter in this contest with stout hearts and with determination to conquer.

The eyes of our families and, in fact, the whole Empire, will be on us once the battle starts; we will see that they get good news and plenty of it.

6. To each one of you, whatever may be your rank or employment, I would say:

GOOD LUCK AND GOOD HUNTING IN THE HOME COUNTRY OF ITALY

B. L. MONTGOMERY,
General, Eighth Army.

July, 1943.

Letter from Monty

war-time importance. Our immediate thoughts, however, were with the show. When we heard it was to be an 'all girls show' there was a mad scramble for seating. It was quite a let-down when several of us failed to get seats. Two nights later there was a little consolation when the A.S.M. and myself went to the 'vehicle dump' to collect two trucks required in Alexandria. We were able to head for the Shafto cinema for a short while after we had carried out our duty.

As if to give us ample opportunity to 'say our prayers' we had yet another church parade on Sunday 27th June. Following this we were permitted for the rest of the day to use the last opportunity for some time to enjoy several hours leave. My colleagues and I headed into Alexandria. At the Ranleh station we 'hopped' onto a tramcar to visit the La Gaita cinema.

On the following morning we had to attend a special parade for a personal address by General Montgomery, Commander of the Armed Forces. His message was hearty but brief. In his compellingly terse style he informed us that very shortly we would become headline news for all our dear family, relations, and friends 'back home'. We, he emphasised in a stirring fashion, would be making the first steps for the Allied Powers to march back into Europe. The freedom of millions would, it became clear, hinge on our heroic efforts. "Good Luck" and "Good Hunting" in the Island of Sicily and the mainland of Europe were but some of his warming, fond wishes for us. In just a short time it would become my turn to put my head into the 'Hatbox of Hell'.

Chapter Six

Sicily Recaptured, 1943.

At the beginning of July 1943 my colleagues and I had to face up to the inevitability of armed combat against one of the most ruthless of armies in the history of the World. I had heard much from my uncle about the resolve and determination of the German soldiers in the First World War. Now, for me, there was no escape from a bitter confrontation against their successors who were probably an equally efficient and even more highly mechanised foe.

On my birthday, 1st July 1943, I sailed with the other troops into Egypt's Alexandria docks. The outline secret plan for our Division was to become part of the Eighth Army. We were then to join a monstrous Armada and to make an amphibious landing at the South East corner of the Italian island of Sicily. Our unit, the Fifth Division, was instructed to land on Amber Beach and take the ports of Syracuse, Augusta and Catania before pressing onwards towards Messina. The L.A.D. to which I belonged was attached to the Fifteenth Infantry Brigade on the Howe Sector, together with the 1st. Battalion of the Yorkshire and Lancashire Regiment and the First British King's Own Light Infantry. These were to be followed by the 'reserve' formed by the First Battalion of the Green Howards Regiment.

My colleagues and I were instructed to board the Steamship 'O Henry' to await further instructions. This vessel was but one of the total of 2,700 – most of these self-propelled and not in tow – that were in the eventual landings. In all they consisted of about one half million tons of shipping.

We were packed on board like sardines and most of us were forced to travel on the decks between vehicles of every

Supply ships with smoke screen in background

description. Whilst there we were somewhat bemused when we each were issued with a booklet entitled 'A Soldiers Guide to Sicily'. We did eventually manage to move about the vessel and make sense of the new currency notes that were also issued to us.

Two days after what I realised might well be my last birthday, we sailed out of Alexandria at 6.00pm. Altogether there were two and one-half troop divisions and some 3,226 vessels of all shapes and sizes. These separated into two main task forces which also included the United States of America's troops. This large convoy was inevitably supported by a protective naval escort.

The following day, American Independence Day, it became apparent to us that the majority of large ships were also crowded with vehicles of every type. For our part, the L.A.D. of the Ninety Second Field Regiment, we were all perched on the top deck and able to witness a remarkable sunset heralded by the 'All's Well'. On 5th July whilst the Mediterranean Sea remained calm we were able to check our equipment and 're-charge our batteries'. Though nothing unusual occurred an overall mood of considerable apprehension had generally pervaded our ranks.

Such a sense of misgiving was dramatically reinforced when at 10am on 6th July the 'Actions Stations' signal was sounded. We did not have to ask 'why' when we saw some of our destroyer class ships encircling our vessel and droping explosive depth charges . We soon heard that the S.S. Shajahan had been torpedoed and sunk by the enemy. After two hours of our 'Stand By' we went onto a 'Red Alert'. Fifteen minutes into these emergency procedures we were ordered to 'Stand By' with our life jackets on as many of the warships commenced firing their Ack-Ack guns. An hour later we had to take cover when the Ack-Ack firing re-commenced. Finally at about 10.15pm. we were relieved to find our ship was still afloat as the 'All Clear' was sounded.

On our fifth morning aboard our ship the sea was calm amidst the hot and humid weather. About 2.0pm. we had a further scare as we were instructed to 'Stand By' as raiders were sighted some way off. Amidst the ensuing flack one of them appeared and then disappeared into the sea. It was an eerie silence that enveloped the whole ship. One collective thought seemed to transfix the entire assembly of my comrades – "what else lies ahead of us and

L.C.I. (Landing Craft Infantry) heading for Sicily. July 1943

will we survive?"– Such thoughts occupied but seconds of our experience but paradoxically seemed to transfix us for an eternity.

As if to reinforce our apparent inability to steer our own course 'in life' we entered into all enveloping banks of fog, the following day. The sea being calm it seemed like an unreal scene from one of the historical Holywood films, or seafaring epics. Any thoughts of the experiences of Captain Ahab in 'Moby Dick' or similar epics were dispelled when about 8.30pm the S.S Bizerla joined us having sailed out from Algiers.

To help calm any nerves or restlessness a general rum ration was issued on the night of 9th July to help induce the last pre-battle sleep. Unfortunately in the early hours of the following morning the Mediterranean Sea appeared to react to our heavy trespass through its territory and whipped up a tropical style storm. So roughly did the sea raise itself that the Garrison Commander advised the troops that no beach landing could possibly be made on that night. A postponement had to be considered but when the assault did finally go ahead I remember how it seemed that each man aboard our ship was in fact grateful that it was so. The overall plan for our operation, code named 'Husky' was to land the USA Seventh Army and the British Eighth Army, on 10th July, on the south eastern corner of Sicily. Both armies were to be almost side by side. The latter was to take the ports of Syracuse, Augusta and Catania. The former was to take Marsala, Palermo and the northern coastline.

At this point in time I imagine that very few soldiers on board would have chosen to join the navy given the choice between that and the army. Our inability to develop the 'sea legs' needed, despite having by now travelled hundreds of nautical miles, was acutely felt. At 1am. on the morning of Saturday 10th July the deafening roar of bomber aircraft engines was heard directly over our heads. Suddenly their silhouettes against the clear moon that night was quite clear. Fortunately, we were soon assured that the aeroplanes were 'friendly'. As our ship rocked with savage ferocity our main concerns were that our vehicles and our stomachs would remain on deck! It was to be four hours later after the bombers had passed us by before we noticed fairy lights in the sky. Some fifteen minutes later numerous gun flashes could be seen over the land as the warships also began to fire their guns.

By 6.30am. as the armed ships escorting our troop carrying ships began to bombard the enemy's shore positions. We each realised that our turn to stand overlooking the precipice of eternity would soon be upon us. From this point there was to be no turning back. No excuses could be made for the ills of mind or body. Each of us, like the enemy awaiting us ashore, had to give our best effort to subdue our opponents or perhaps we would never live to see the outcome of our exertions.

A cacophony of incessant sounds and the frenetic outburst of movements in the discharge of unrelenting warfare ensued. The first distinctive sounds I recall were those made by the unleashing of the Royal Navy's Nelson and Sixteen Inch Monitor Guns. These bombardments were vent against those of the enemy that occupied crucial shore positions. As the Allied

Invasion of Sicily. July 1943

Transport and stores landing on Sicilian coast. 10th July 1943

Airborne Divisions touched down their commandos ran ashore to begin their efforts to subjugate the deadly, large coastal guns. In concert with these intrepid fighters a single first wave of the Fifteenth and Seventeenth Infantry Brigades clambered down the scrambling nets and into the large landing craft vessels to pursue their hazardous, specially chosen routes ashore.

How welcome a sight to all on aboard our ships was the wave of Spitfire fighter planes which flew directly above us at 7.30am. Some thirty minutes later our ship moved close enough to the shore to allow us to see the progress of the vanguard of landing craft. These doughty vessels were jammed full of men and vehicles searching out some beach space.

As I 'stood by' to witness some of my colleagues enveloped in this mad scramble I captured a series of memorable scenes in my 'mind's eye' that I was never to forget. Some of these I have retained as flashbacks that still recur in my memory some fifty years later. I am unable to erase, for example, my recollections of enemy Stuka dive bombers launching their deadly explosives as many of my colleagues jumped from the landing craft and landed on the sloppy, sand-covered beach.. One of these sticks of bombs fell only yards away from the bow of a nearby craft. As I waited, for what seemed like an eternity, another wave of enemy Stuka dive bombers arrived and released a further stick of bombs almost in front of our ship's hull. Without a second thought I found myself dashing for cover under one of our ships Ack-Ack gun platforms. The throb of my increased heart beat seemed to be almost in unison with the rapid rhythm of shell fire from the Ack-Ack gunner.

Our good fortune during two close shaves suddenly changed, however, when our ship shook violently as the next stick of bombs fell upon its rear end. The almost immediate death like silence from the gun above me indicated that the gunner above me had also become a casualty in this attack. When I climbed to help him I saw that his arms and his hip had been hit by shrapnel. Medical aid did eventually arrive but the severity of his injuries, after basic first aid was administered, was great. The harsh cruelty of war further came home to me when I later heard that the hospital ship he had been taken to had also become a victim of the campaign and been badly hit. Unable to escape from the wrath of yet another wave of dive bombers the hospital ship was eventually sunk. Although many planes were shot down by our Bofors, or Ack-Ack guns, the continuity of the raids throughout daylight hours of the 10th July left me a bag of nerves. I remember as my mouth kept 'drying up' that it was one of the most parched days of my life. Before the day was out, meanwhile, the Fifteenth Infantry Brigade landed upon 'Howe Beach'. This had been marked as 'mine-free' by the large streamers of white-tapes that had been laid down by the Royal Engineers.

The stress of battle conditions continued throughout the following day. As early as 4.30am. an air-raid alarm was sounded and we all had to 'Stand To' with life jackets on again. One of the hellish enemy dive bombers at this point scored a 'hit' and sunk a nearby transport ship. The resulting flying shrapnel spread across our ship and wounded some of our gunners and other nearby personnel . When I heard that five wounded had been taken to one of the hospital ships in the bay – denoted as such by the large red paint cross on its side – I simply wanted to get off the boat and get ashore as quickly as possible.

The early hours of the morning seemed to be favoured by 'Gerry' for his air-raids because at 4.45am. on the 'Glorious Twelfth' the ships sirens shrieked once more. As still more Stukas flew over us again yet another transport ship was hit and burst into fire on her forward deck. I remember how 'lucky' she seemed to stay afloat after this ferocious attack.

It was many hours later, at 11.45pm. that my chance to leave my vessel came at last. I received orders to climb overboard and down the rope ladder to an awaiting landing craft. Aboard this smaller vessel was the 15cwt. Bedford truck I was to drive ashore. The driver originally assigned to the vehicle had been wounded during one of the aircraft attacks on us.

The uncertainty of our fate was fully brought home to me when yet another air-raid alert was sounded. This forced us to lay alongside our transport ship for the rest of the hours of darkness and then into the daylight beyond. I recorded in my diary "What

15 cwt truck landing in Sicily

a place to leave us. We certainly have a grandstand view of the ferocious activity". I felt at times that I must been dreaming but the reality of this very real nightmare could not be denied.

Once again I entered the unlucky day of the month, 13th July and at 8am. dive bombers flew over us yet again bringing the usual response from our Bofer guns. As I lay crouched beneath my truck a shell exploded alongside our vessel. After a seemingly endless wait, until 10.00am., my relief was unforgettable as I heard the instructions to 'move off'. Landing on the shore, and alighting into about three foot of water, we drove between white tapes along a makeshift track. This quickly led us through an orange grove to our main route. A right turn brought us on through Avola where we made contact with our main L.A.D. group.

Farmhouse in Sicily July 1943

Once more, fortunately, we then encountered some friendly faces. After a sharp left turn into a little side road we travelled up a straight incline to a farmhouse. Here we confronted a gathering of several Italian families who at first were terrified for they believed it was our intention to shoot them. After we had allayed their fears they befriended us and graciously treated us to some of their own wine and to simple but tasty food. Our welcome respite here was quickly brought to a close by our Armament Sergeant Major. He had received orders that we had to move on to Syracuse. It was further revealed that several important bridges had been damaged by the enemy and replaced with temporary R.E. Bailey bridges. That evening we made an overnight stop just at the rear of a battery of Ninety Second Brigade's twenty-five pound field guns.

The following morning, from 8am. these guns were 'opened

up' to pound away at those enemy positions in the locality. Soon after this opening barrage of shells we witnessed numerous Sherman tanks passing us on the roadway. The tanks, we heard, were moving to new positions just behind our field guns. As four Stuka bombers flew over us at very low heights we heard our guns continue their attack. We also heard 'on the grapevine' that our artillery was firing at close range upon those nearby enemy positions that were just beyond us in the so called 'death valley'. Additional news also reached us that we were shortly to come face to face with the Herman Goring Division as we slotted in behind a vanguard of our own advancing troops.

If the 13th of July 1943 had seemed unlucky then the 15th became unforgettable. To this day – some fifty years after the events of that day – the scenes my comrades and I witnessed became imprinted indelibly in my memory. The morning was reasonably peaceful to begin with. Little of note happened before we left our rendezvous position at 3.00pm. that afternoon. As we cautiously moved into the deep ravine, or 'death valley' we witnessed the destruction of several historic bridges. Worse was to follow. Further on we saw our first major carnage in this arena of war. We came across one of our tanks that had been struck by the enemy's armour-piercing shells. The effect was sickening for the shell had passed through the vehicle and the crew's mangled bodies lay strewn across the scene.

Very nervously we had to make a short stop a little further on from the mayhem. We quickly referred to our official ordnance map of the area to plot a way to our next meeting place, Villa Samundo. About 11.30pm., being able to still make use of the bright moonlight we underwent a further harrowing experience. As we came upon a former local radio station we were soon able to see that it had been rendered useless by the enemy's shelling. What came home to us most strongly as we moved on was the aroma of death that pervaded the eerie atmosphere that had enveloped this station.

It was absolutely necessary to stay alert whilst passing through such places as 'Gerry' had littered the area with 'booby traps'.

Such was the strain demanded by our heightened concentration that it inevitably exacted its toll. One such experience for my colleagues and I happened in the early hours of 16th July. We had continued our convoy journey northwards when we were suddenly forced to a halt. Our chosen route had been blocked by yet another bridge being destroyed and an alternative way forward had to be found. It was eventually decided that our group of vehicles and their troops should pull off the road and wait in an adjacent field. During this pause a body of Royal Engineers began to erect the necessary Bailey Bridges.

These circumstances, we now fully appreciated, were significantly different from those we enjoyed in our homeland preparation 'excercises' at Formby, near Liverpool. In these Sicilian battle arena circumstances our entire convoy was forced to make an 'about turn' to re-negotiate a suitable route. Our L.A.D vehicles, as usual – being at the rear of the convoy – were to be the last to move. It was to involve us sitting and waiting for more than an hour before our turn to move off came. The wait proved too much for us. The strain of being constantly on the alert for more than twenty four hours caused us all to fall asleep!

When I awoke with a start, about 3am. that morning, the main

Recovery crew with Austin and Leyland truck,
Sicily 1943

body of the convoy had moved off. I quickly went into the field and aroused my 'sleeping comrades'. By this time we felt the convoy's main column was well ahead of us. In our frantic attempts to reach it we exposed ourselves to additional dangers. As we stopped at one road junction to examine the wheel track patterns we suddenly came under fire. 'Gerry' we believe 'opened up' his 88mm. guns on our 'lost patrol'. What must have been one of the most unceremonious scrambles in the war resulted from this. Fortunately all the vehicles in our party had some distance between them so as soon as the firing began it seemed that our drivers jumped from the vehicles without waiting for them to come to a halt. In the ensuing great dash across the fields to a nearby woodland some even lost their footwear. How times had changed, we later mused, from those dignified mass charges at the enemy during the First World War!

Eventually, after the firing had ceased, we returned cautiously to our vehicles. After much heart-searching we finally regained control of our nerves, and cautiously moved on through Melilli and Sortino about 7.00am. that morning. By 9.15am we had reached Lentini where, much to our relief, we joined up with the main column and finally came to a halt at its rear once again, I collapsed into a weary sleep at the back of the Dodge truck.

My respite, however, was soon interrupted by the strafing of our vehicle by aeroplanes directly overhead. Even in such dangerous moments some of us still managed a grim smile. On this occasion it happened as I scrambled from the truck. I leapt across the road to scamper onto a grassy verge and dived under our large Leyland recovery wagon. Beneath this vehicle I met our Sergeant Major, Mr. Sheriff. From the distinctive smell of him I soon realised that he had the misfortune of throwing himself into a healthy portion of cow dung as he heroically leapt for his life! In later times he became known, or referred to, simply as 'Smelly Sheriff'.

Such confusion though not everyday was quite common in the ever changing conditions we encountered. Later that day, for example, it was reported that German paratroopers had landed in the vicinity. Having positioned ourselves at one side of a large square-shaped field we were unaware that, about the same time, other allied troops had set up camp about several hundred yards opposite to us. We realised at daybreak that these men may well have mistaken us for the enemy in the dark if we had not been so quiet in our assembly there. This we thankfully regarded as a disaster averted.

The respite period in the shelling activity however, was only short-lived. At 1.30am. the following day we were startled by the terrific noise created by the sudden barrage of shells unleashed by our corps guns. A further deafening explosion followed half an hour later. The nearby German paratroopers had set fire to a farmhouse about half a mile away. This, it was assumed, had housed their ammunition stores in this district. It was eight hours before we were able to reach the site and explore the enemy workshops that were still standing. This was a dangerous activity because we had been warned about the possibility of 'booby-traps'

No casualties occurred in this search operation but this was not to last. At 10.30 pm. as the sun was setting, low flying Messerschmit fighter aeroplanes strafed our ground positions. Our corps barrage returned the fire – using about 200 guns that each fired 100 rounds per gun. We heard Gerry has suffered some heavy punishment but we also learned that we too had suffered many casualties. In this tense, frightening and worrying situation we managed to sleep but little that night.

Our anxieties did not recede because an almost inevitable series of counter attacks occurred on the next day. As a party of us travelled into the Forward Area of the battle we were attacked once more. We had been instructed to drive the recovery wagon to hoist one of our trucks from a ditch when it happened. Almost without warning a half-dozen Messerschmits swooped down and strafed us. As we dived for cover we heard the crackle of our Eighteenth Light Brigade using their Ack-Ack guns. On this occasion we were informed that they had shot down three or four of the enemy air craft. It was later recorded that they had established a military record in fact by shooting down a total of 31 aeroplanes within one week of our landing in Sicily. By 6pm. that evening we were keen to get away from this district as quickly as possible. There was a general sense of muted delight as we moved off for a new rendezvous point some two miles away. Unfortunately, at 11pm., two of my comrades – known as Paddy and Hoyle – were shot at by German troops and suffered chest and arm injuries.

There was to be no respite, however, we soon realised that the stench of death was to linger for several more days. When we moved off on 19th July, we pushed ahead across the exposed Catania airfield. The pungent smell of decay from dozens of dead and rotting cattle was inescapable throughout the entire low lying plain where the air-base was sited. Matters were made worse when we came upon one of our infantrymen who was rambling and wandering in a confused state. When it was diagnosed he had a form of 'shell shock' the A.S.M. instructed me to lead him to the rear of our Dodge truck and try to make him comfortable. By the time we reached a Medical Officer, several miles further on at a First Aid Post, I myself had become predicably disturbed by his predicament. Further air-raids upon our position during the dim light of dusk did little to calm my attacks of nerves and general state of depression.

The pattern of an early morning attack by both sides continued during the early hours of the next morning. On this occasion at 2am. our gunners opened up, using their '25 pounders'. with a Divisional barrage of shells. Once again they unleashed 100

25 pounders in action 92nd Field Regiment RA Sicily 1943

rounds from each gun. It was about 3am. or 4am. before we managed to get some sleep.

Fortunately the next day, 25th July, was a relatively quiet one and we were able to billet in a deserted farmhouse. This day also, we learned later, was the one on which the dictator Benito Mussolini was to fall from power and put an end to any organised Italian resistance. General Eisenhower was anxious to hasten a complete Italian surrender and to secure a bridgehead in mainland Italy. This was to be centred near Naples in an area large enough to draw to the south as many German divisions as possible. For our part, life on the farm continued when we moved to a new rendezvous near Lubiata and its nearby aerodrome. Here using yet another farmhouse as a base we carried out routine maintenance and repairs. Top of our list was the need to check over each vehicle's starter- motor, dynamo, regulator and ignition systems.

On 26th July our 'sojourn' in the striking Italian countryside was curtailed when we moved on to the former barracks of the Italian army just beyond San Anastasia. We soon discovered why the buildings were more commonly collectively known as the 'flea pit'. Having stopped at the site three of four of my comrades made their way by foot into a large hay and straw filled barn. I remained with another party of men to examine the exterior of this building. Without warning the indoors party suddenly evacuated the barn and ran out shouting, waving their arms and then slapping themselves all over their bodies. Without a second thought they began to strip whilst some of the onlookers dashed to fill buckets with water. As they were doused unceremoniously we could easily see that they were covered from head to toe with flea-like insects. We humorously compared their antics to those of the comedy film stars such as Charles Chaplin, Laurel and Hardy etc.

Such light-hearted moments helped to relieve the tenseness of our situation. During the next five days we heard news of air-raids on the towns of Augusta and Syracuse. It was particularly disturbing on 1st August when the day and night

Primosole Bridge: Captured by 1st Parashoot Brigade

were filled with the continuous sound of heavy air-raids on the two towns. On the following day the shelling continued but we managed to occupy ourselves by attempting to repair a small radio which we had found in our farmhouse base. When we finally did succeed in repairing it we were unable to locate any English-speaking radio station. Our thoughts then turned once more to coping with the sound of all-day heavy artillery fire. I never needed much encouragement to offer a daily silent prayer for deliverance from this dreadful situation.

When news did leak through to us we were pleased to hear that Allied bomber air-craft raids had scored a major success nearby. On 3rd August we had heard terrific explosions not far from us. They had lasted all night and the sky had been brightly lit for the same period. It transpired that our air-craft had had direct hits on a German ammunition train in the railway sidings at Domino near Gerbini.

Soon after we had to move to a new position and this too was adjacent to a railway bank. When we reached the site, near Benante, North of Carmito more violent explosions could be heard in the direction of Mount Etna. On the 5th we were informed that after a long struggle Catania had been taken by our troops. I and my colleagues continued our 'rural ride' and moved into yet another farmhouse. On this occasion it was at Toscane near San Anastasia. Another serious threat at this site was malaria, in this district we were warned that it was prevalent and we readily took the special tablets of Mepachrin and used the anti-mosquito bed nets whenever possible.

Whenever possible we were only too happy to undertake any opportunity to relax. Unfortunately it was a natural tendency to overdo it if given the chance to do so. In my case this happened during the evening of 7th August. Having been granted a mini-leave period, George, Dougy and I joined an Italian family in a bout of wine-drinking. Although the drink was an everyday Itlaian beverage at meal times anyone unused to large amounts could soon find themselves becoming tipsy. When we eventually returned to our farmhouse, just after midnight, George was merrily singing away in his finest broken Italian. He particularly caused us to laugh with his phrases such as "Stacio get me the Moonio". Stacio was his nick-name for one of the memorable sergeants from headquarters. As the moon moved rapidly in and out of the night-time clouds, this seemed a particularly humorous idea for our intoxicated 'lads'. Though I had enjoyed only a small amount of 'vino' and had also eaten a large meal I had begun to feel uneasy on our return to base in the Dodge truck. As a fearful headache developed, and I began to feel very sick, I felt my recently taken dose of Mepachrin had added to my violent reaction. Though the discomfort lasted only a few hours it did heighten my awareness of the perils of the demon drink!

On the 8th August we moved on yet again to another rendezvous some four miles south of Belpasso. Here we were able to attend a most welcome 'concert' during a lull in the fighting. One character in the cast, bearing the name Belpasso Bertie – named after the town – raised our spirits by his special brand of humorous song.

The charm of this show business personality was still in our

Monty: Fag issue

minds when on the following day some of us met another man who became destined to become world famous for his military expertise. At 9.50am. having just moved to a further rendezvous point we stopped in a field alongside the main roadway. As we looked down the road from where we had travelled we saw a large white convertible saloon car approaching. Within moments the car drew alongside us and stopped. From the front passenger seat a distinctive officer stood up to address us. It was none other than General Montgomery or 'Monty' as he was more familiarly known to us. He chatted with us for a short while. I remember how he emphasised to us that we were "on the road to victory". After specifically encouraging us with the words "keep your spirits up" he handed out cigarettes to each of us before he moved on. To meet and speak personally to a man who was to become a living legend was a tremendous boost to our morale. We felt stronger in spirit for those few never-to-be-forgotten moments in our life threatening situation.

This period of rapid movement across Sicily continued its momentum when on the 10th August we moved to rendezvous about one mile north of Borrello for a short stay. At 2pm. that afternoon we moved off to San Alfio and on through Nicolosi and Pedara. It was here that by chance I met two members of the Army Film Unit – both cameramen – who had lived quite close to me in Liverpool. As their homes were in the Fazakerley district close to my own home we each had much in common to talk about. They camped overnight quite close to me and so I was able to talk with them at length about one of my main hobbies, the cinema.

Though they moved out on 12th August the day became memorable for two major events. Firstly, A.S.M. Sheriff went into hospital for dressings to his light shrapnel wounds. Next, after we had moved to yet another meeting place we met with a terrifying surprise in the early morning hours. Unknown to us we had moved within range of a newly mounted Allied 5.5inch heavy gun battery position. When the guns opened up without warning we were shaken violently in our beds by their outburst. They had been so cleverly camouflaged that we had not noticed these newly commissioned weapons when we had moved into our base. Such was the power of these 'Howitzers' they could fire their shells up to a range of some eight miles. Perhaps these monstrous weapons had symbolicaly heralded the growing confidence of our forces. After hearing them we could not but

Figure 55   5.5" Howitzers, Sicily. July 1943

help reflecting on 'Monty's' wise words about being on the road to victory. By 13th my colleagues and I had been withdrawn from the action. The news that Gerry had been forced out of the island of Sicily and been forced back onto the mainland 'toe' of Italy was greeted with glee by our men. Even Sergeant Major Sheriff returned with a smile, with fresh bandages, from the hospital on 15th. With the eclipse of the moon that evening some of us hoped that it was also a symbol of our growing military successes over the enemy. Heavy air-raids were nevertheless still unremittingly conducted across the Straits of Messina which separated Sicily from the mainland.

What a poignant moment it was on 17th August 1943 when we heard that all fighting on 'our' Italian island had ceased. An eerie silence suddenly pervaded our ranks. The peace and quiet of that day lingered long after in our memory. It helped to stimulate our resolve that we would fight for the complete freedom of mainland Italy. This new objective was now to become the next target in our Odyssey.

Two examples of leaflets dropped by Germans to destroy morale

Chapter Seven

From Southern Italy to the Adriatic, 1943-44

Two days after the fighting ceased in Sicily we were busy preparing our vehicles for the amphibious assault on the Italian mainland. The overall strategy for the Fifth Division – still part of the X111 Corps of the Eighth Army – was to cross the Straits of Messina in Operation 'Baytown'. Our divisional units were then to trek through Southern Italy and to join up with the American Fifth Army after its Naples' landings.

By the 27th of August the efforts of our aircraft to 'soften up' the enemy positions across the Straits of Messina began in earnest. On that date numerous air-raids from Catania were begun by our 48 twin-engined bombers. Whilst the air crews, using Gerbini airfield as their base, flew on their missions we took our last opportunity for some light relief before we attacked on the ground. Somewhat ironically we attended a mobile cinema performance organised by one of our anti-tank units. The title of the main film was 'A Yank at Eton'. We heard on the following day that some 51 North American bombers and their crews had flown at 8am. from Gerbini. We could not help thinking of the contrast of their life-style with that enjoyed by the film hero at Eton. This day, being Sunday. we went to a well-attended church parade in a large field.

By the end of the month, on 31st. August, we began the movement out of our base as the first stage of our invasion strategy. Travelling through the badly damaged town of Catania we took the coastal road. This enabled us to see clearly the battleships, Nelson and Rodney, – armed with 16inch guns – sailing into positions just south of Reggio Calabria. Their mission was to bombard the fortified enemy positions on the mainland coastal areas. The effectiveness of their exertions was to be

Boarding landing craft for invasion of Italy. 1st Sept 1943

reinforced by their armour-piercing high explosive shells each weighing about one ton. In all we travelled some fifty one miles to our new position..

When the month of August in 1943 finally came to an end, we were able to reflect just how little we had been able to relax during what had been a traditional holiday period in more peaceful times back home. As we suspected September, too, was to be an unforgettable month. The first-day began with more Allied bombers flying to the mainland to continue the assault waged by H.M.S. Nelson and H.M.S. Rodney. Our role was to lay in wait to board those landing craft made available for our part in the main invasion.

On 2nd. yet more of our bombers moved across the Straits of Messina as two more battleships, the Valiant and the Warspite, helped reinforce the huge artillery barrage against the enemy. This combined American and British assault was reinforced on the following day by a Division of Canadian soldiers. This day, we were later realised, was the fourth Anniversary of the start of the Second World War. At this point in time a common unspoken thought amongst soldiers from both sides must have been 'how long can this nightmare continue?'. The first allied troops to set foot on mainland Italy on this historic day were the British Fifth Division. Followed by the Canadian Force they managed to land at several positions around the historic town of Reggio. Fortunately, though 'Gerry' managed some retaliatory air-raids against them they proved largely ineffective.

Yet another of our 'great moments' came on 4th. September. We left our camp and went directly to a beach position where, at 1pm., we boarded the landing craft that were to sail to the mainland. Within half an hour of climbing into these craft we moved off and eventually landed about two miles to the south of Reggio itself. There after a march of about one and a half miles from the beach itself, we came upon our assembly area. Here it was our nerve-wracking experience to await the arrival of our vehicles. My unit had been told to expect two Austin stores lorries, a Leyland recovery truck and a Dodge truck. The A.S.M. and myself were to take charge of the latter.

This I clearly recall seemed like one of the longest days of the war to me. We were ordered to sleep in an open field, with only a nearby orange grove as protective cover. We had no form of bedding, or blankets and no supply of food other than our crude emergency rations. As we confronted the discomfort of intense heat by day and extreme cold by night we also had to contend with an enemy air attack from dive bombers about 4pm. As we unhesitatingly ran for cover beneath a bridge that spanned a dried-up river bed, some four to five casualties were incurred by our main party which had remained at the principal assembly centre in an adjacent field.

By the 5th we had turned into a band of 'scroungers' as we searched for food after we exhausted our meagre rations. Fortunately, when we finally located the main assembly depot we built a make-shift fire. Using only small bundles of twigs and other dry wood we were able to heat some tinned bacon and beans. Whilst our only 'afters' were dried biscuits, known to the troops as 'hard-tack', we had to make do with liquid refreshment by drinking from a small stream.

When we made our way into Reggio at 5pm. for more food and blankets we found the town largely deserted except for troops. Some wounded civilians had been forced to remain and were attended too whenever possible by one of our medical units. Our own general frustration and despair seemed to be symbolised, about 11pm. that night, by a violent thunderstorm. This in turn also forced us to scatter for the welcome shelter afforded by yet another bridge. About 3pm. when the storm receded we finally managed some intermittent sleep.

This respite was soon shattered by the sound of innumerable vehicles, loaded with equipment, landing on the beach to await their instructions to move on up to our 'front line'. It fell to our party meanwhile to approach a nearby power station and search for any signs of life. This rather large installation – which appeared to house two giant rectifiers capable of an output of 3,000 volts – had apparently been used to provide the local railway lines with their source of traction. If it was so, and there was no reason to doubt it, the Italians were extremely well-advanced in this type of electro-technology. When our mission had been completed, without any form of opposition from the enemy, we managed to return to our initial position and use a railway bridge once more as a cover whilst we bedded down in the evening. Once again, however, any prospects of uninterrupted 'sweet dreams' were hindered by yet another air-raid. Beginning at 9pm., this attack was met with a return of fire in the form of the heavy Ack-Ack barrage discharged by our Eighteenth Light Ack-Ack unit.

Even more vehicles and equipment were disgorged onto the beach for our support on the following day. It was quite heartening to see both Sherman tanks and large supplies of petroleum and ammunition being stock-piled on the beach. Both Landing Craft Transporters and the amphibious, four-wheeled barges 'or DUKWs' managed to land their cargoes despite a heavy rainstorm that began at 9.30am.

We had only been on the mainland for just a few days when a BBC and Rome Radio 'news flash' was given to us. At 6.30pm. on the evening of 8th September we were heartened to hear that the Italian's fascist led army had formally surrendered to the Allied powers. Local Italians greeted this information with frenzied rejoicing. When we entered the nearby villages church bells were rung and 'the locals' invited us to share their wine-drinking celebrations that included dancing in the streets. For our part we still managed to enjoy ourselves despite the evening darkness being pierced by the Verney lights and Ack-Ack gun flashes. We also heard that by this time our Fifteenth Infantry Brigade had encroached as far as Goia.

This rising tide of good fortune continued for several days. On 9th September, for example, we heard reports that British and American troops had landed at the port of Taranto. We remained level headed about such information because at the same time it was also common knowledge that such advances had met with strong German resistance, particularly at Salerno. This type of bitter-sweet conditioning of our attitude to the progress of the war became more palatable for us the following day. At this point we heard Persia had decided to declare war and to support our efforts in fighting the German Army.

In the afternoon, about 2.30pm., we experienced yet another unique event in that ever changing war-front arena. A concert was arranged on the Amber Beach and noneother than George Formby, that much admired and highly famed film star and comedian had arrived in person to 'top the bill'. In his inimitable jollyness he seemed to push back the imminent, life threatening forces we were to face. Like so many of his own courageous 'show biz' peers his was a courage that was so unique and perhaps largely underestimated at that moment in time. As he effortlessly reeled off his seemingly limitless repertoire of 'smash hit' songs – such as 'When I'm cleaning windows, Leaning on a Lamppost, Hi Tiddly Hi Ti Island' and many others – the welcome strains of his ukulele seemed to dispel for a few magical moments any despairing thoughts about our fate.

By the time George had performed his morale-boosting show

L.A.D. Tea break   *Bailey Bridge*

the Vanguard of landings at Salerno were progressing as
planned, after very stiff opposition and many casualties. Two
days after his show our L.A.D. vehicles were also landed from
Sicily. They had been transported across the straits of Messina
with the other vehicles of our Regimental Headquarters. In a
strange way we were glad to collect them at their landing point.
By now we fully appreciated how much quicker and less
arduously we travelled in them compared to the foot marches we
had had to undertake when laden with full kit. As soon as we
took charge of them we intensified our preparations for a long
journey northwards. Once again Bill Wignall checked to see that
we each had an ample stock of emergency food rations.

We finally moved out on 13th day of that month of September,
hoping that this would not prove as 'unlucky' a day as some had
already been in our army life. Having journeyed out of Reggio,
in Calabria, our convoy went at a steady pace along the western
coastal road Yet again we were grateful that the Royal Engineers
had advanced in front of us constructing vital Bailey bridges to
offset those stone ones which had been destroyed by the enemy
in the attempts to delay our progress. To cross quite a few of these
temporary constructions was a time of considerable anxiety
because they traversed steep ravines that fell away hundreds of
feet at a time down to sea level. For any of our colleagues who
dreaded sharp bends around cliff edges it was a nightmare
scenario. Fortunately, we were able to punctuate such fears by
idle chatter about the many small towns and villages to be seen

perched high in the mountains or on scenic hill-tops. We also joked how fortunate the inhabitants of such highland fortresses were to avoid the threat from the mosquitoes that were known to make their homes in the stagnant waters of the low lying valley bottoms. For my part I managed a wry smile as our truck passed through the region of the western part of the 'toe' of Italy made famous by Palmi, Rossano, Monteleoni, Nicastro, Amantea and Montalto – the latter of which I knew to be renowned in a scene from the Opera 'I Pagliacci'. Situated in such a mountainous terrain this was an area that was regarded as too difficult to sustain a substantial 'battlefield' conflict of the type we had experienced to-date. This was a region that I felt – because of its own vigorous and rugged grandeur and by its own natural inbuilt defences – would not encourage destruction and devastation by contemporary war-mongers.

By the middle of the month our lofty mountain tour was curtailed as we entered, about 14th September, into a route that took us back to more level ground. This was short lived for at 6am. as we left our rendezvous point in this region we began to move once again up a steep hill that housed this part of the coastal road. When we descended from this stretch of road we made an unexpected halt at midday. We not only had time for a meal but also for an equally unexpected chance to 'lay down our arms' and head for a welcome swim in the sea. The benevolence of the decision to allow this period of relaxation stemmed not from the military desire to 'fete its heroes' but simply because our route north to Belvedere was known to be strewn with bombs! Though the bombs were timed by the enemy to explode principally under those bridges to be used by the Fifteenth Infantry Brigade they were systematically and painstakingly diffused by the Royal Engineers. It was sometime after our swim before we were able to appreciate the value of the debt we owed to the bravery of the bomb disposal experts.

Such was the inbalance of the fortunes of war that whilst we frolicked like tourists in the sea our brother soldiers ahead of us to the north were being heavily counter attacked. At Salerno, where these events were being enacted, our Fifth Army brethren were having a very difficult time. Though it was our mission, as an integral part of Montgomery's Eighth Army to race to the north to help relieve the pressure on the Fifth, we were unable to do so at that moment in time.

When we were finally able to move on and pass through Belvedere we shortly afterwards turned inland to negotiate a mountain pass. This feature was to lead us, after eight difficult miles, to a small deserted village sited in a small valley there. Yet another piece of good fortune occurred when the small party of two or three 'scouts' sent out to reconnoitre the deserted buildings returned, at 11pm., with 'abandoned' bottles of wine. The chance to enjoy yet another civilian luxury in the form of our own 'wine party' was regarded as a further benevolence too good to miss. Fortunately, there was not enough 'vino' to tempt us into any serious dereliction of duty.

By this time we calculated we had travelled some 87miles from Reggio. Not having visited 'home' for more than three years there was now a fervent desire to return to see those people and places we had left so long ago. For many amongst us it took but little by this time to distract us into those thoughts and feelings which had been largely for so long subjugated by our a military way of life. On 15th September as we passed through the village of San Sosti we underwent an experience that seemed to summarise many of the sacrifices we had made in the war.

We felt we had to stop on the road when we saw a small Italian boy dash excitedly into the awaiting arms of a man we assumed was his father. It appeared that the adult had managed to find his way back from a forced labour gang near the German front lines. As they hugged each other uncontrollably we had a 'whip round' and managed to come up with a bar of chocolate. When the boy was handed this prize he unleashed his hold on his father and screamed Grazi, or "thank you" with great delight. At that moment his eyes beamed with elation and tears began to pour from them. Even as hardened war veterans, which we now felt we had become, we found our own eyes welling up with sympathy. With this one act of kindness and its unsought after reaction I realised how dreadful and calamitous the war had been for millions of ordinary folk throughout the world. My especial thoughts were also to recognise how the children in particular had suffered. Many of us did find some consolation later that day when, at 3pm., General Montgomery paid us yet another most welcome visit. Once again the opportunity to meet him at close range was a magical moment for me. His unique calm and quiet jovial, attitude served to raise our spirits at that time. Yet again he offered cigarettes to those he chatted with.

When we left the village of San Sosti at 7am. on 16th September we returned along our previous route for a short while. Whilst heading back through the pass to Belvedere our good fortune continued in abundance. One of the bridges we had to traverse had been found to be 'alive' with bombs. Fortunately the master timer on the bombs must have been faulty and the Royal Engineers were able to diffuse the threat. When we reached the coastal road we headed for Maratea and then went inland to another mountain pass that had to be cleared of any pockets of Italian resistance fighters. About midnight, having journeyed some seventy miles through Lauria, Treconina, Rivello, we arrived at San Rocozzo the headquarter's rendezvous for 'B' Echelon.

The following day at Vallo we joined up with other forces bound for Salerno. Firstly we had to wait as a strategy was devised to rid one of the route's railway tunnels of an obstructive German machine gun crew. Our 'answer' to this opposition was unfeeling, accurate and deadly. One of our seventeen pounder guns, affectionately known as The Pheasant, was moved into position at 'our' entrance to a long straight railway tunnel. Our gunners released their armour piercing shells – with their eerie whistling sounds – through the tunnel. The effect on the Germans manning the machine gun nest was immediate and uncompromising.

Having methodically rid ourselves of all such opposition we were now able to advance to a new rendezvous on each of the days ahead. On 18th September several of the German Mark V

92nd Field Regiment 25 pounder in action. Italy 1943

tanks were put out of action by our seventeen pounder, anti-tank guns. This helped the Fifteenth Infantry Brigade to arrive at Lagonegro at mid-afternoon on the same day. As we moved to our new rendezvous, about six miles into a heavily wooded district, we heard reports that our Spitfire aeroplanes were supporting us by patrolling the region. Reports even came through that the First Battalion of Green Howards ahead of us had pushed on and crossed the River Noce.

Such news, though a fillip to us, was always greeted with caution. This was especially relevant on 19th after we had moved out at 6.30am. for yet another new rendezvous point. When the Fifth Reconnoitre Regiment headed towards Sala Consalina it clashed with the rear guard of the German 26th. Panzer, or Tank, Division. Here at least two British armoured cars were 'burnt out' and two British Troops killed.

The steady destruction of bridges by the Germans continue to delay us as the Royal Engineers raced against time to construct their replacements with temporary Bailey bridges. It was whilst we awaited their completion of one of the latter that we stopped on the main Brienza road and had yet another memorable experience. While we were waiting at a military road block a neatly clad, Italian twelve year old boy emerged from one of the deserted 'pill' or gun-post boxes. Looking rather frightened he approached our truck and burst into song.

Italian boy who sang to us

His rendition of Santa Lucia was a revelation and a joy to listen to. The beautiful sound and clear arti- culation of his words was wondrous. The 'lads' and I were trans-fixed by that youngster's vocal achievement. Almost without thought we collectively showered him with sweets and chocolates when he had concluded his fine performance. In return he was visibly shocked and suddenly dashed over to our truck. When our reaction to his impromptu act had sunk in our spontaneous appreciation also induced him to seek refuge in our truck. I will never forget the smile that spread across his face as he joined us. Unfortunately he instantly came to see if we might 'adopt' him but he had to be handed over to the Italian police, or carabineri, at the next town we passed through.

We surmised that he had been parted from his family during the mass evacuation of the low lying towns that had been so heavily shelled during recent months. Before we left him we managed to take his photograph near a beach. After his departure we remained at the site for several hours before moving out to a new location. This time we went via the ancient city of Padua to meet at the central railway station in Brienza.

With so much urgency involved in continually 'moving on' there was never a dull moment. Each day my fellow soldiers and I realised that this could either be our last or that we might meet with a terrible calamity. On 21st. we joined with the 'B' Echelon some two and one half miles South East of Brienza. Little did I realise at that time just how close to death I was.

Blown Bridge: Roccamofini. Italy

About 6.30am. A.S.M. Sheriff left us to travel to Belvedere for essential vehicle parts held in stock at our base stores unit. It became my responsibility whilst he was away to oversee the repair of a B.S.A. 500cc. motor cycle. When the news came through that we soon had to move out quickly I had to ride the 'bike' on to the Regimental H.Q.

For me this was to be a most confusing mission because when we had moved out at 4pm. through Brienza our convoy had been held up at the site of yet two more heavily damaged bridges. Our diversionary route had then taken us through nearby fields and then under other bridges and along a dry river bed. By the time I had mounted the repaired motor cycle darkness had descended and my only guides were the white tapes lade down by the Royal Engineers.

As I fully appreciated, the tapes indicated that the route within them was clear of explosive land mines. Still travelling cautiously, however, I came face to face with near disaster at 3.40am on the morning of 22nd. September. It came as I suddenly negotiated a slightly muddied path with a very steep ascent. So marked was the upward turn of the route that I almost took the 'bike' into a somersault. Being in darkness I missed the correct 'turn off' on the bank and went straight into an adjacent river bed. Suddenly an exasperated, booming voice bellowed out at me "Where the hell are you going?" This yell of a military policeman ended with his stark declaration "You are in a minefield". My retort was crude but understandable in the circumstances. "Oh Bloody Hell!". I blurted out. What a relief it was when I managed to successfully re-negotiate myself.

It was not only myself who had difficulty in negotiating a way through that additionally hazardous part of our route. The twenty five pound field guns we were transporting in our convoy had to be hauled up the bank I had strayed onto. Unlike myself the guns were slowly moved by several bulldozers specially introduced for this difficult task. Thankfully by 5.30am. the convoy was again able to proceed in a more orderly style on a level route through woodlands beyond the troublesome bank of earth. When we finally reached the B Echelon base I was most grateful for a few hours rest. "Thank God for that being over" I remember uttering to myself as I fell into a weary sleep. This longed for rest did not last for long. On the morning of 23rd., by 8am., we were on the move, yet again. This time we were to head for the Regimental Headquarters Base some six miles ahead at a meeting point that was itself about one and a half miles south east of Picerno. Here we were able to enjoy a short period of combat inactivity away from the type of front line hostility we had come to expect. We again occupied ourselves with routine repairs and maintenance on 24th. September. Reports meanwhile filtered through that the 45th United States Reconnaissance unit had met up with our beleaguered Fifth Reconnaissance patrol. The latter had been heavily mortared in their positions to the south of the township Castel Grande. On the same day the Green Howard units had been ordered to return to Picerno. We realised that it would not be very long before we would be once again ordered into action. This seemed to be reinforced by yet a further report that the Green Howards infact were regrouping for a counterattack when the time was ripe.

There was a slight delay in these plans when we met with a

sudden heavy downfall of rain. Though the prolonged cloudburst restricted the initial movements of the Green Howards 'they' received the order to 'go' on 26th. Before we could join in any major attack we had to overcome a series of problems. Our Dodge recovery vehicle had to be repaired on the 27th so we took a replacement on loan. The next day there was a further heavy thunderstorm – which brought fierce winds and a deluge of rainfall – this began at 9.30. in the evening. Within an hour our bedding, which was on the ground alongside the Dodge was being soaked through our leaking canvas 'roof'. Though we moved our bedding to a drier place by 2am. it seemed hopeless as the storm increased in intensity. With violent bursts of both thunder and lighting suggesting we were experiencing a near 'tropical storm'. A.S.M. Sheriff wearily got out from under his bed covers. Cursing profusely, as he began to 'bail' the water from his resting place, he decided to head for the dryness of the Dodge's cab. Though there was insufficient room to 'stretch out' I decided to join him. For the remaining few hours we sat in the cramped seating and rested as best we could.

When the storm abated, about 4.30am. I was unable to prevent myself from uttering the comment "who said we had come to sunny Italy?" Fortunately the late morning of the final day of the month was very bright and enabled us to carry out all the necessary 'mopping up' operations. There were inevitably some 'winners' and some 'losers' in this situation. Though we were quite easily able to dry out our wet clothing we were unable to prevent some of our 25lb. guns from becoming bogged down in the muddy tracks. To free them we had to use our Leyland Recovery and some tractors which we borrowed form local farms.

We felt in these circumstances that we were not really sorry to see the end of September. We hoped that the new month might bring a rapid increase in the number of days of good fortune. Secretly I suppose we were hoping that a miracle might occur to bring the war to an end overnight. It was of course not to be, and, unknown to me at that time I and several of my close comrades were to have further close encounters with death.

When we heard on 1st October that the Allies had marched into Naples our spirits were raised. In broad terms the Fifth Division had come under the command of the Fifth Corps. At the same time our immediate progress was again hindered by the heavy rainfall throughout the 3rd. and 4th of that month. Still based at Picerno it was so bleak at this time that we were allowed a ration of brandy with our supper time drink of tea.

Four days later we moved out of Picerno and attended to several transport breakdowns that occurred on the route through Potenza, Tolve, and Irsina. Almost like tourists, we stopped on the road near the latter to watch in curiosity as some local villagers crushed vast quantities of grapes which they had harvested for wine-making. It occurred to us that hopefully at the same time our forces were finally helping to crush their German oppressors.

For the next few days in fact our progress through the Italian Peninsula seemed to gather in pace. Having successfully arrived at our rendezvous – five miles beyond Gravina – on 8th October we moved rapidly the following day through Spinazzola, Minervino, Canosa and Foggia. To reach our next rendezvous we searched for a point that was to the west of Foggia and six miles south of Lucera. We eventually arrived there, at 6.30pm. on the 9th October.

This was yet another of our farmhouse 'stop overs' and we left it at 7am. the following morning. This and the following day marked the beginning of a period of intense personal danger for myself and my immediate associates. Our convoy had just moved through Lucera and San Severo when it had to make a left turn first before Seracapriola. At this point the Ninety Second Field Regiment went into action. Overnight we stopped in a woodland near a road junction. There was little sleep for me that night, however, for I was instructed to move out to repair a faulty regulator on one of the Bren Gun carriers.

Having been aware of the rather exposed nature of my position I was more than happy to return to the main convoy. It moved quickly on some five miles to the new 'B' Echelon rendezvous position one mile east of San Croce. Here, like boys from a school, a small group of us went searching in a local field for 'fresh' potatoes. We did not regard this as petty theft because this rural area had largely become deserted by the exodus to safety of the locals. Alas we could only eventually make chipped potatoes – with no traditional and much loved fish in batter – to add to our 'bully beef' and tinned peas.

Though this incident excited us enough to compare it with some of our boyhood escapades we were soon brought back to reality. We suffered two casualties; a gunner known as Culliford was killed, and a soldier surnamed 'Davies' from headquarters was badly injured in a mortar attack on our position. One of the explosions occurred close to the parked recovery wagon I was in and it flung me across the cab. This, allied to the heavy rain throughout the day, made the situation somewhat unbearable.

This engagement in 'close-fire' was a preamble to the heavy fighting that was to take place on 12th October. The Lancashire and Yorkshire Regiments became engaged in a fierce battle with the formidable 88mm guns of the enemy. In return our Ninety Second Artillery unit used its guns to pound away at the positions of the enemy throughout the day. The Sappers for their part went ahead to clear up to twelve miles of road which had been 'booby trapped' with land mines. To help counteract the delaying tactics of the enemy five more Bailey bridges had to be constructed and a further ten route diversions planned.

Though there were many sacrifices and acts of heroism performed in the line of duty it was usually only the most outstanding that captured our imagination. One of these occurred on 13th October when Sergeant Lamber from 'D' Company of the Lancashire and Yorkshire Regiment stormed four enemy gun posts. Fittingly, he was later awarded the Military Medal for his deeds.

This day, I also remembered as being somewhat 'lucky' for me. Not only did Italy renounce its former allegiance to the German forces it also declared war on it too. Next, when I was called upon to mount a fixed gun tower to rectify a fault with a starter motor I had another 'near miss'. Whilst I lay on my back attempting to re-install the disassembled motor a large shell from one of the enemy's 88mm. guns landed on the road a short way from my position. Needless to say I was content to stay put for some time before returning to my main post.

Despite the increasing warmth during the day it was beginning to grow noticeably cold by night. As a consequence we were pleased to welcome any change to our mundane food rations, particularly if it warmed our 'insides'. One such remarkable alteration happened on the following day. Firstly we were granted an issue of one bottle of beer per man. After several months of being deprived of the chance to enjoy a visit to a 'bar' this was welcomed. Next, the L.A.D. managed to purchase a local pig for 250 lira, or for about 50p. in modern terms. The animal was of course dead when it reached Bill Wignall, who was still our 'chef' and he made tasty use of it. Though not officially trained as a cook – being a dispatch rider in his army role – he came to be respected by us as a man with great culinary 'expertise'. When he was later transferred to join the 13th. Infantry Brigade we certainly regretted it.

The appalling weather meanwhile continued when, on 16th at 2pm., we moved on for a new location north of Bonefro. Here whilst we were billeted in a derelict garage we learned that on the previous day our lads in the 13th. Infantry Brigade had suffered severe casualties. It did not really surprise us when we heard that quite a number had been caused by the insidious booby trap practice of attaching trip wires to land mines.

Fortunately, on the 18th matters improved after our regional headquarters moved. Not only did the weather become more tolerable we learned that one Corporal Pears had been awarded the Military Medal for dragging a wounded member of his patrol, whilst under fire, across the Biferno River. The following day we too were able to move off, at 3pm., to a new location near the San Croce railway station some three miles south of Casacalenda.

Here we enjoyed something of a return to a civilised existence when the NAAFI, (Navy, Army and Air Force Institutes), was able to make 'fresh issues' available to us. Here they treated us to cigarettes, chocolates, a series of toiletries and numerous other luxuries. What a delight it was, too, to be issued with new underclothing after an unclean existence whilst on the move for such a long time.

Our rest in this oasis of high living lasted only four days. Then we moved out and travelled through Campobasso and stopped overnight in a field some two miles east of Ferrazzano. In this and the following night we were to be subjected to the constant noise of heavy gunfire from the Ninety Second Regiment. I lay in the back of the Dodge throughout both nights and did not sleep for any length of time. This need to be 'on the alert' continued for me on 27th. when I was ordered to drive a motor cycle to our Command Post to repair an ammunition truck. Though the truck's electrical system was failing to 'charge' I believe I must have 'charged' as I executed the repair in almost record time and returned 'at full throttle' on my motor bike.

Throughout such dangerous periods in our army life we tried to keep our intrinsic sense of humour. This was to emerge in many different situations, in many countries and at many times. One prime example I recall happened on 28th October when the Regiment moved on yet again. This time we travelled only a short distance because the rainfall was heavy throughout the day. When we finally pitched camp in a roadside field we set about foraging yet again for 'fresh' potatoes. On this occasion we made more chips in our small 'cook house' and quickly made up a rough notice announcing "Come and taste our Speciality – A Muddy Chipolato". We also added the words "Italian style; Toast and Ice Cream for 'afters'".

This ability to laugh in the face of adversity undoubtedly helped pull us through the bleakest moments. When we moved out on 29th October from Campobasso to a further location in an open field our site should have struck terror into our hearts. Across the field were numerous deep bomb craters often some twelve feet deep. Here was a stark summary of what the enemy could do to us. Fortunately such was our resilience and determination to overcome our ruthless enemy that it did not deter us. When we finally settled in for the night, some five miles south of Bojano, I fell asleep once again in the back of the Dodge truck. On the last day of the month our sense of expectancy rose,

L.A.D. Cookhouse in Potato field

too, as we clearly heard our aeroplanes bombing Gerry in his position about six miles beyond Bojano.

As November began we moved further onwards to the south of Bojano a well-farmed district. Here I had the opportunity to move out of the Dodge at night and sleep in a deserted farmhouse. Once more I was unable to resist speculation as to where the owners or occupants of the house might have moved to. My general impression was that they had moved out to higher ground in the valley and were living 'rough' or with friends or farming neighbours there. As we realised only too well the civilians often paid in full measure for the disasters of war.

On 3rd., at 5am, there was an unusually heavy barage of the enemies positions by the nearby units of the Ninety Second Brigade Artillery alongside those of the Ninth and Ninety First. Finally, after much heavy fighting, Sernia was taken from the Germans. Unfortunately many civilian casualties had resulted from the substantial bombing operations.

It was our turn to move some six miles south of Isernia at 10am. on 7th November. On this occasion our new 'residence' was to be a large house by a railway line. After a stay of some five days we travelled on to a railway station further 'up the line'. It was fortunate that by this stage in the war very little caused us a major surprise. About 1am on the 12th we were not unduly shaken by the sudden roar of a 'ghost train' carrying vital ammunition and

'F' Type Elec w/shop lorry   *Bonefro 'San-croc'*

general supplies. Needless to say it was regarded as vital to move such invaluable goods under the cover of darkness whenever possible.

We certainly experienced a lengthy period of foul weather at this time. On 15th we took our Leyland Recovery vehicle to rescue a series of our quads, or mobile guntowers, that had had to be abandoned owing to the inclement weather. Two days later we were called out to rectify a distributor fault on a Bren gun carrier. Needless to say the persistent rainfall caused numerous additional electrical faults in many of our vehicles. On 23rd we had to attend to the giro control on the gun turret of a Sherman tank. This problem had also resulted from the damp in the sodden climate. The following day, mercifully, our regiment was withdrawn from action to 'rest up'. At this point the quest for the capture of Cassino was being waged – only twenty miles to the west of our location; we were having an easier time compared to those engaged in that struggle.

When we were moved back, on 25th November, to our previous location to the south of Cantalupo it was something of a relief. We stayed at the town's railway station and were blessed by a day long absence of trains – possibly because it was risky to run them in daylight when they made such large targets to the enemy. Apart from the nuisance of having to undertake light duties we were able to experience some organised entertainments that occurred over a period of several weeks.

On 25th November we were given the opportunity to visit a mobile cinema in Cantalupo. It was a pleasant surprise to see the performances of a star-studded cast in the famous film 'Casablanca'. This Warner Brothers production, starring Humphrey Bogart, Ingrid Bergman, Claude Raines, Sydney Greenstreet and Peter Lorie, was to become one of the most popular films of that era. The charismatic performances of the film 'stars', with the immortalised lingering melodies of the theme tune – As Time Goes By – was a welcome fillip.

As we entered December we began to think of the season of Advent and some of the Christmas customs we had enjoyed 'back home'. We did have some relaxation, on the first day of that month by attending a concert organised for us at Biaro by an anti-tank unit. Ten days later a number of us were invited into a local Italian home to enjoy some of our hosts chicken and wine. After undertaking a workshop written test on 11th I and several comrades were invited into yet another house. To my delight on this occasion we heard some Italian classical singing using an old '78' gramophone. With plenty of 'vino' to hand we were invited to join with the community style singing which was ably supported by several mandolin and violin playing 'locals'. Being so far away from home and being in the teeth of war this was an unusually relaxing and pleasant experience.

Meanwhile in the Adriatic Sector both the Canadian and the New Zealand units were subjected to heavy fighting. To give them additional strength elements of our Division were released to that Sector. We were included in this movement and were to head towards the sizeable town of Lanciano, with an uncomfortable move on 11th December.

When I received a second typhus inoculation on 13th. I was unable to carry out rifle duties because of the resultant pain. Nor were my spirits raised by the news that the German 26th Panzer Division and Sixty Fifth Infantry units had become active in the region with their mortars and artillery. Two days later, however, I did receive the welcome news that I had passed the recent Trade Test Paper. With this as my excuse I went out to celebrate drinking local vino.

This small good fortune came to an end on the following day when we had to move on to Palmoli. This was a small town with a well-known monastery some ninety miles away. Here we were billeted in a derelict building near the side of a main road. We suspected for a time that it had its own ghost when we heard a groaning sound emerge at regular intervals from the cellar. It was something of a comic relief when we finally discovered that the suspected spirit was none other than a resident donkey housed down there.

Meanwhile the news from our nearest 'front line' was that the Green Howards had come under heavy shell-fire on 19th December. We heard the following day that some 9,000 rounds had been fired in the previous few weeks, by the One Hundred and Fifty Sixth Field Regiment. It was at such moments we were grateful when by comparison to some of our artillery units we had to undertake only general maintenance duties.

We were in fact able to see distant gun fire 'flashes' as we moved during the night. This happened, for example, on 22nd December as we moved through Gissi to camp at Palmoli. Passing over numerous double banked Bailey bridges we stopped from time to time to rest and were able to see this type of action in the distance, near Casalaguida.

Two days before Christmas we continued with our own 'pilgrimage' to within one and a half miles north of Lanciano. We stopped at yet another farmhouse and this was close to our field gun positions. In the appalling weather, our heavy vehicle movements cut up the terrain into acres of mud and slush. Such handicaps called for intrinsic single-minded resolve by all of our men. Some soldiers inevitably went beyond the call of duty and showed defiance of the enemy by their singular acts of heroism. Such was the case when Corporal Hill of the First Green Howards who was badly wounded but continued at his post to repair some of our broken communication lines. For this he was awarded the Military Medal.

Lanciano, Dec 30th 1943

By Christmas Eve such was the extreme cold of that winter that Lanciano became covered in snow to a depth of two feet. There was no 'goodwill to all men' when, beginning at 4am., the 10th. Field Regiments and the Fourth Brigade Regiments, began firing what was eventually to total some 130,000 rounds. Throughout the fog-filled day sleet fell from time to time. In the evening there was something of a respite for us and we managed to join with a farmer, his wife and their family and chat in English whilst seated around a log fire.

We could never be sure how that Christmas Day might be celebrated but how glad we truly were when some parcels began to arrive for us. We had a festive dinner inside a barn and were fortunate to have turkey, roast potatoes and green vegetables followed by traditional pudding. Though we believed there was to be a temporary truce we did hear some heavy gunfire throughout the day.

Any doubts about the safety of our position were dispelled on Boxing Day by heavy barrages fired by both sides. In addition some fourteen enemy bomber aircraft dived towards our position with such intent that we unhesitatingly took to the cellars for refuge.

As snow continued to fall in the Lanciano region we heard, on 27th, that there was still an abundance of activity in the skies above us. Nevertheless, despite such intimidatory action we opted to accept an invitation that afternoon to a Divisional Concert Party organised by the 'Low Gang' of the Ninety Second Field Regiment. The show was of the 'Grand Style' since it took place at the local Opera House. In truth it did go 'with a bang' – especially when a live 17cm. enemy shell landed and exploded at the rear of the stage. The show was hastily abandoned. Since there had been no heating, in the theatre we were able to leave at 'full speed' because we were still wearing our overcoats whilst seated in 'the stalls'. There was therefore no need to stop at the cloakroom on the way out!

When we eventually moved into Lanciano itself, on 29th, my party was billeted in some flats that had been formerly occupied by local doctors. The enemy shells, had no respect for anyone and when a 17cm. shell landed only 100 yards from our 'digs' two of our lads were killed. There were many 'hits' throughout the town and we were rigidly shaken by a bulletin that announced a local cinema filled with many children had been another casualty of this dreadful war.

Despite these trying circumstances we attempted to make some 'observation posts' on the roofs of the billets. It was re-assuring, therefore, to hear that our bomber air-craft were making concentrated attacks upon the German positions in and around Ortona and Orsogna. More enemy shells landed in Lanciano, about 10.30pm. but thankfully by this time the town had been evacuated.

By New Years Eve we had moved some two to three miles outside Lanciano. About 7pm. we attempted to organise the start of our seasonal celebrations. Borrowing an old piano from a heavily blitzed building we began our small-scale community singsong. Some of the locals joined us and when the opportunity arose they sang some Neapolitan songs in their own inimitable style. When midnight arrived everyone joined in to sing the traditional favourite 'Auld Lang Syne'. For several hours after the 'party' a deathly quiet persisted almost eerily. About 3am. on New Years Day, 1944, the heavy guns of the enemy opened up once more with all their former ferocity. At such a highly emotional time and in such life-threatening circumstances the one unspoken thought for our group and thousands more must have been 'what will the New Year bring?' This simple question surely must have pervaded the minds of both friend and foe alike.

Battle map: Italy invasion (Southern Italy) 8th Army 5th Division

Chapter Eight

Anzio Beachhead and Rome's Release, June '44.

When the New Year, 1944, did arrive the War had entered a critical phase. Whilst our efforts in Italy had helped to push the enemy's forces half way up the Italian mainland a major offensive, viz 'Overlord', was being planned by the Allies in NW Europe.

The latter was to have important repercussions for our efforts in Italy. Firstly, General Montgomery had had to leave 'us' at Christmas when he was called upon to play a crucial role in Overlord. Secondly, any possible reserve troops available to us were to be withdrawn for the NW operations.

Several attempts in Northern Italy, meanwhile, had been made by the Fifth Army to dislodge Kesselring's German divisions from the Hitler Winter Line across the Garigliano River. It became only too apparent at the beginning of the new year that the projected Eighth Army advance from the Adriatic had become bogged down in that difficult terrain to the north of Ortona and Lanciano. The upshot of this was that the Eighth Army was now to 'pin down' the enemy in this region and the big push, or 'left hook,' on Rome was to be undertaken by the USA Fifth Army. To add more weight to this USA impetus the Fifth Division was to be secretly transferred from the Eighth Army to the Fifth.

Before he left for home, however, General Mongomery was to pen and publish the following tribute to the Fifth Division:

"I would like to tell you how very sorry I am that the Fifth Division is leaving the Eighth Army. During the campaign in Sicily and Italy the Division has fought magnificently and has played a notable part in the successes that have be achieved. I have always known that any job given to the Fifth Division would be well and truly done. It is a first class division in every respect, and I hope we may all meet again soon. Good luck to you all"

The first day of the New Year, 1944, had seen my comrades and I return to Lanciano and we undertook a welcome change in our usual form of billets. We moved into a rather modern Mansion house which even had sufficient parking space for us to leave our vehicles at the rear. About this time I began to feel the first painful twinges of a nasty toothache but I found time to write some letters home. As I wrote to my mother I recalled how I would even have welcomed a visit to our 'home' dentist. It was the home style of life I missed very much rather than the 'terror' associated with a Liverpool dental journey!

I also noted how heavily the snow continued to fall, on 2nd January, and that I could no longer bear my oral pain and had to 'report myself as sick'. After the necessary extraction I returned to my new digs and received some mail from home. It fell to me soon afterwards to re-commence my general vehicle maintenance duties. By night the short respite from the shelling by the enemy ended as he 'opened up' once again at 11pm. On this occasion five civilians were killed.

When we finally moved out of Lanciano, four days after these fatalities, we heard that the north Italian war front had become a 'stalemate'. We, meanwhile, wended our tiring way to the south and crossed the River Sangro. This point on the river had been the site of a recent fierce battle. Our path led us on some twenty four miles to that Western Front of the War just north of the Torino-Di-Sangro railway station. The next day we went significantly further on, some eighty five miles in total, passing through Vasta Termoli, Serracapriola and San Severo. We reached the latter in a state of exhaustion just before midnight.

If we felt that day to be trying we certainly did not bargain for the journey we made a day later. On this occasion we convoyed 107 miles, through Lucera, Ariano, Grottaminarda, Avelino and

Monteforte. Though we had travelled further and the weather was extremely cold we still managed to reach our destination about an hour earlier than the previous day. By this stage, however, the continuous shelling of the region by both sides had a noticeable affect on the roads. On the 9th January our progress was restricted by the large shell craters along the route. When we finally reached San Giuliano, via Cancello, 263 miles from Lanciano, we had a serious degree of sorting and re-grouping of vehicles to carry out.

As fortune would have it I and the A.S.M. were sent about eight miles to collect supplies from Naples. Our 'shopping list' included food and spare parts for our vehicles. Back at base we continued to experience mixed fortunes. On the 13th, after we had returned we were astounded to see about one hundred and fifty Flying Fortress bomber-aircraft heading north. These we later discovered were to pound the German positions in the historic medieval monastery at Monte Cassino. Their passage above us, about 9pm., was a vital element in the Allied forces major 'push' to free the ancient city of Rome from German occupation. The earnestness of the Allied resolve to strike an emphatic blow in Rome was further brought home to us some three days later. Just after midday we witnessed yet another huge formation of Flying Fortresses heading towards Cassino. We heard on the following day that in one Allied attack, on the Gustav Line, some 1000 rounds had been unleashed over two days. As a direct result, Monteforte was taken by the Allies on 18th January.

On the ground there was a similar degree of heavy fighting. This continued all night, on 20th, in Tremonsuoli. When the Second Royal Iniskillins went on the attack they suffered many land mine casualties. Amongst the distinguished acts of heroism at this point was that of Major Tanner who was awarded the Military Cross.

By now reports were coming through that an unprecedented major effort was being planned against the German positions across the region. There was a realisation throughout our ranks that a surprising co-ordination of our forces was being brought about for a vital attempt to deal the enemy an insurmountable blow. It came home to us in the last week in January that the 'big push' to free Rome would incorporate a large reinforcement of forces specially draughted into the area to ensure the Allied efforts did not fail. At this point we heard that two officers of the Ninety Second along with many in other ranks had been killed as the Fifteenth Infantry Brigade had taken over the Argento Sector

Our first precise news of what might happen came via the reports that we read in our Eighth Army 'newspaper' on 21st January. It became clear that there had been an abnormal build up of Allied ships in and around several ports in Malta, Sicily and Naples. Those off Naples were especially interesting because little by little we began to realise that these would make more large-scale landings at the beaches of the port of Anzio a near certainty. Quite simply if the Allies could win control at that point then access to Rome the heart of the ancient Roman Empire – some thirty seven miles further on – would be within their grasp.

What initially appeared to be a very simple plan, was eventually to account for a very high cost in its execution. All that was believed to lay in the path of the Allied invaders at this time was a detachment of the Herman Goring Panzer (Tank) Division and a hotpotch of enemy artillery ranging from the odd 8.8cm. Anti-aircraft to Italian, French and Yugoslav field guns. The opportunity to proceed immediately and without a significant loss of life was missed. As a consequence the name Anzio was to haunt many brave men who eventually had to fight frenetically to keep this vital beachhead.

On 22nd. January when the first forces of the Americans and British made their joint landings in ideal weather conditions there seemed very little enemy opposition and the bridgehead was comfortably seccured. The Royal Navy together with the U.S. Navy landed 36,034 men, 3,069 vehicles and some 90% of the assault equipment of the U.S. VI Corps. In these were included the British First Division and the American Third Division, a regiment and a battalion of paratroops, three battalions of Rangers and a brigade of Commandos. Later these were reinforced by units of the British Fifth Division. In the course of these initial landings, losses amounted to 13 killed, 44 missing

The Beachead, Anzio

and 97 wounded. The landings were also supported by four light cruisers and some 24 destroyers. These helped to silence the German's shore batteries and permit two German battalions which were on the beach to be overrun.

The German's opposition to this invasion appeared noticeably on the 29th when the weather broke with a gale force wind. The enemy forces reacted violently using their glider, bomb-carrying torpedo planes, their 88mm. and 170mm. shells and mines in the sea lanes. The surge of Allied troops towards Rome was unduely delayed and the enemy, under Field Marshall Kesselring, used this invaluable time to forcefully organise his response to the landings. The net result was a most horrendous conflict.

Reports of widespread heavy fighting were to filter through to us over several weeks. We heard on 22nd. that on the Garigliano Front the Lancashire and Yorkshire Infantry had suffered heavy casualties. On the following day we heard a very heavy artillery barrage from the Allies had been matched by 'Gerry' returning fire with his 17cm. Howitzers. With a total of eleven counter attacks being beaten off it fell to us to repair the many vehicles that suffered damage.

It was whilst we were in a new location, in a farmhouse that Gerry shelled our position again, on 27th. Most of these attacks, fortunately, landed some way away from us and mainly at a local important road junction. The next day there were shell bursts over the top of the hill to the east of the nearby town of Castleforte. This continued for several days and was particularly heavy in an all-day bombardment on 29th. The following day came the chilling news that our Division had been warned that it would have to move to Anzio to relieve the British Fifty Sixth Division as quickly as possible.

It was not until 2nd February that the Division, through its representative Major General Gregson, was able to reach the beachhead to see the reported horrors there. On the same day I, too, experienced this anxiety of coming under mortar fire when I was sent by motor cycle to repair a fault on an anti tank truck.

Needless to say I used the 'bike' to travel at break-neck speed along the damaged roads. Three days later when our 365 and 367 Batteries were heavily shelled there were many casualties. Our L.A.D. was busy for almost a week after recovering their damaged vehicles and doing everything possible to get them moving again. Our trips to sites of the broken-down vehicles was often harrowing. Some of the enemy's mangled bodies lay strewn across many of the routes we were forced to use.

Any break from these most desperate of duties was most welcome. On the 16th. February we managed to travel into Sessa for a mobile film show. By coincidence the following day two photographers gave us a briefing of what they had filmed at the battlefront. They stayed in our camp for a while as they gathered their material for showing in Great Britain. These brave men had a simple but dangerous routine of staying with us before they moved up to the front to take their film. After their short stay with us they quickly returned to their main base at Naples before returning 'home'.

Our repair duties continued to take us from one dangerous place to another. I still however, unlike the professionals above, had to content in taking film 'stills' with my small camera which was less sophisticated than their equipment. On the 20th we moved to workshops in a field park at Marzano. The next day we moved to Mignano which was only four miles to the south of the

ill-fated monastery site of Monte Casino. When we moved even nearer the next day – just one and one half miles away – we witnessed at first hand some of the tragic bombing of that historic monument. Flying fortresses flew in by the score but despite unleashing their horrendous explosives they seemed to have but little effect.

L.A.D. group Marzano

On the 23rd February the intensity of the battle to take the hill site began in earnest. During the next six nights we had little sleep due to the ferocity of action by the opponents there. On 29th we moved out of San Vittfore – making our way to the west of Mondragone on the coast. Although we were billeted in a first floor flat, which had a holiday aura because of its unusual balcony, we knew it was no 'rest-camp' we had landed in. Here we were instructed to prepare for our turn at the Anzio beachhead. We were to become part of Major General Gregson Ellis' promise to relieve the beleaguered Fifty Sixth Division.

In the week prior to this it appears that conditions at the beachhead had deteriorated. The Salient had been 'wiped out' and the First Division had fallen to half of its original strength. The degree of allied sacrifice was reflected in the large numbers of dead and wounded that were reported to be spreadeagled across the entire site. Several regions therein such as Buonriposo Ridge, the Factory Area and Carroceto – had been captured only to be lost again as the Germans managed to regroup – and counter attack with singular effectiveness. The conditions that had to be endured there by both sides were horrendous. As both freezing rain and heavy shell fire burst upon the troops they had to cling to their muddied ditches with the utmost determination. In just one single act of heroic defiance Major Philip Sydney rose from his jammed machine gun and hurled grenade after grenade at the advancing foe. This he did despite being injured in both legs at the time. Such courageous action was to earn him the award of the Victorian Cross. Deeds similar to his were not rare it would appear at this battle. So great was the intensity of the fighting from both sides that it was regarded by many as being as ferocious as that witnessed in the defence of Stalingrad by the Russians.

As February came to an end it became clear that this winter was to continue as an unforgettable one to those on both sides who survived it. On 3rd. March we handed over the vehicles we had repaired and we then left Mondragone. Early the following day, about 7am., we boarded the convoy trucks that were to take us to Pozzuoli, to the north of Naples. Here we boarded a corvette or a destroyer and wearing life jackets sailed to the north through an exceptionally rough sea. Such was the foul weather we experienced that I was but one of many who was desperately seasick whilst 'en route' for Anzio.

When we arrived, 5th March, at 7am. many of us felt so rotten that we were unable to appreciate the dangers posed by the 170mm. shells that were bombarding the port. When we eventually went ashore we were transported to a coastal rendezvous point about five miles to the north. This, the area for the assembly of the Fifth Division, was situated adjacent to the Ninety Seconds 25lb. gun emplacements. Our 'thank you' for relieving the Sixty Fourth Field Regiment was a concentrated burst of shelling form the enemy's Eighty Eight's.

Perhaps this single-minded attention from the enemy should have awoken us to the fact that we had taken part in what was to become regarded as one to the most controversial landings in the War. Originally designed to achieve a victory within a week it was in all to take some four months to achieve it. Our operation

Hospital Ship (Anzio Bay)

required pinpoint planning – with some 70,000 men and 20,000 vehicles landing before dawn – and had to be reinforced by a considerable array of cruisers, destroyers, mine sweepers and submarines, What perhaps had been underestimated however, was the resolve of our foe to resist our efforts. The 'price' for our part was very high for 155 officers and 2,838 men from our Division paid with their lives in this struggle for supremacy. The 'price' paid by the enemy was even greater for some 25,000 graves were eventually left to mark their part in the battle.

The entire drama of Anzio was often later referred to as 'The Hatbox of Hell'. This term it appeared had first been used with regard to General Montgomery's role at the desert battle of El Alemain. Before the latter there had never been a major Second World War victory for the British Army. After that time the tenacity of our forces appeared so resolute that we were determined to win whenever we engaged our foe and at whatever the cost. If only for the change in our attitude to the War, therefore, the 'Hatbox' had fired us to never again contemplate anything other than victory.

Day after day our resolve seemed to harden. On 6th. my colleagues and I 'set to' and we dug out our own deep trench to take cover in. We had hardly completed our task when a fierce shower of Anti-Personnel bombs landed in our midst. These explosives each hit the ground before bouncing approximately a further six feet and then exploding. The following day both sides unleashed their artillery for long periods.

This type of attention from the enemy made our crucial maintenance tasks even more arduous. It was three days later, for example, when a group of us attended a faulty starter motor beneath a quad tower that we had another close-escape. Without warning an 88mm gun opened fire at us and we could only crouch in a dug-out corner, expecting the worst. Two days later we came under heavy shelling throughout the day. We had only been a week at the beachhead by this time and yet it was totally unlike any beach 'back home'!

What we had been led to believe might be a short stay at the

Bomber brought down in Anzio Beachead, Italy.

beachhead in Italy was to continue as a nightmare experience that continued through March, April and even into May. On 14th. March a number of enemy aircraft – 35 FW 109's and ME 109's – attacked the beachhead and they seemed to head to the eastern or American sector. When we were at last able to leave our dug-out during a lull in the shelling we realised just how lucky we had been. Just a few yards away from us was a large hole approximately ten feet deep. Though we remembered a heavy thudding sound had been heard nearby during the attack we had not realised how much the soft earth close to our position must have absorbed the main force of this particular explosion.

Compared to our plight here, however, the experiences of the German 'inmates' at Monte Cassino Monastery must have been even worse. On 15th. March the news came to us that the Flying Fortress bomber aeroplanes has more or less obliterated that noble medieval building by their dropping of 500 tons of bombs.

We were by no means safe though because two days later, at 4.30am. we came under attack once more. When it began I dashed to take cover in a tunnel that ran under a nearby road. In my panic I tripped and snapped some of our telecommunication lines. As soon as possible I reported my 'accident' and though these breakages were soon repaired I ultimately heard that a hospital in our district had suffered many casualties as a result of the shelling.

In view of this doleful information I felt no remorse when it was reported that three German fighter planes had been shot down by our Bofors or quick firing, light anti-artillery guns. A further 'sting in the tale' was that these enemy aircraft had been chasing a 'flying flea' – the small aeroplane which was specifically used to observe large-scale enemy activity.

We had to remain a 'captive audience' for most of the aerial dogfights. On 20th, for example, several spitfires were engaged in a fight to the death with ME 109's. Some of the latter suffered

Anzio (entering dug-out)

fatalities and when the enemy began to re-shell our positions we too paid a similar price. Captain Knowles was killed together with several of the gunners from our base.

After this period of high anxiety for us we settled down to about five days of relative calm. Without warning on 25th. March it all began again. I was walking to our cookhouse situated just over a small hill, when the 'pop, pop popping' sounds re-commenced. Within seconds several 88mm. shells landed on the opposite side of the road to our dugout.

In an attempt to reduce the threat from these shellings some of our heavy calibre guns were moved in – just behind our entrenched positions. When these newly sited weapons were fired the enemy immediately replied with heavy shell 'air-bursts' over them. Two days later when our battery of 7.2's fired another volley of shells at 'Gerry' there was again a tit-for-tat reply by the opposition.

This trial of strength continued on 3rd. April when at 10.30am. a vehement ground attack was made upon us. This was a deliberate and sustained attempt to drive our troops back into the sea. We had been prepared for this eventuality and had been ordered to sleep fully clothed in case we had to move out quickly from the area. My feelings throughout were very mixed for though on the one hand we had a bren gun mounted on our Dodge truck, on the other I was unable to swim! Fortunately, although the enemy's noisy air-raids lasted several hours our counter-attack was eventually successful.

At the same time the repair duties of myself and my colleagues continued. On 4th April we went out to attend to a tank that had become immobilised through a fault on its starter motor circuit. Two days later my good luck, in not being injured by the enemy in the War, disappeared. In one of the fresh and exceptionally ferocious air-raids I received a shrapnel wound in my left arm and had to report to the 158 Field Hospital for examination.

This was not the way I had been used to spending the Easter

period which we had just entered. We enjoyed the hotcross buns we were given about 2pm. on 8th. April but not the anti-personnel bombs dropped in our midst on the same day. Two days later it was even more frightening when we experienced the fire power of Anzio Annie for the first time. This 'nick name' was that given by our troops to a Big Bertha gun on the outskirts of Rome. The gun was reputed to emerge when required from a tunnel and fire enormous 560lb. shells. Its range of fire was estimated as being about thirty miles, the approximate distance we at Anzio were from Rome.

Those shells that came closest to us at this time went just beyond our position and into a 'crowded' military area where both a hospital and an ammunition stockpile were sited. Having by this time been five weeks at Anzio I was more than glad to 'move out' on 11th. April. We were not 'out of it' completely because our new 'home' was to be at the Fifteenth Infantry Brigade workshops. These were one and one-half miles outside the port of Anzio. After just one day there we moved on and went into a new 'dugout' on a cliff edge. The success of the Eighteenth Light Ack Ack in bringing down some eight enemy aeroplanes

Anzio Annie after capture

during their strafing raids of that day brought a welcome lull in the fighting.

After a week of routine repair duties the temporary cessation in hostilities came to an end. On 21st. April the enemy sprung a 'surprise' air-raid on us between 4 and 7am. that morning. He 'paid' for it again when three more of his aircraft were brought down by our gunners. After this outbreak matters did seem to improve. On the following day I completed a form that was to detail my military service since 1939, and it was eventually to bring the award of an Italy 'Star'. This seemed to imply that I would probably be alive to receive the award and it came as a boost to my morale.

In the relative calm of the next four days many of us managed to wash various items of clothing and hang them out to dry. As we joked about 'hanging washing on the Anzio' – not Ziegfried Line – we also welcomed the opportunity to attend another 'professional' light entertainment concert. On 25th. the well known radio celebrity, Winifred Vaughan Thomas, compered the beach performance that was also recorded by the British Broadcasting Corporation.

Our delight at the very good quality of this show gave way the following day to 'gloom' as the heavy rains returned. About 6.20am that morning, following a night of torrential rainfall, our dugout became flooded. The water was so deep inside the trench that some of the buoyant articles – like our boots – began to float between our beds. As water dripped through our sandbagged 'ceiling' it even began to penetrate through the 'walls'. When we received fish for breakfast it became a common joke that these had been caught from our own private pools!

To make matters worse the heavy shelling re-commenced about 11pm. Our biggest 'catch' to-date coincided with this period because some fourteen planes in total were 'hauled' in by our gunners. These gruelling encounters continued so that by 29th., about our eighth week at Anzio, it seemed to have become the norm.

Dug out Anzio   *Bomb Carrier*   *L.A.D. Group*

As we entered the month of May - at home traditionally welcomed for its parades and show of spring flowers – we expected little change in the dogged opposition and counterattack strategies of the enemy that we had grown accustomed to. The first week was somewhat quieter, than its predecessors and only three planes were shot down. By the second week, however, we could again hear our formidable friend, Anzio Annie, was performing strongly once more.

It was in this week, particularly after 11th. May, that our fortunes changed for the better. Having received a fresh issue of 'summer wear', a light 'Khaki drill' uniform, we attended an enlightening lecture from Generals Alexandra and Clarke. Their message was that all units both inside and outside Anzio were to prepare for a major offensive. This was to be the 'push' to capture Rome from the enemy. It transpired that 11pm. was the 'zero hour' to begin this historic battle and by that time we had all been issued with additional arms and ammunition. Now for us it was a matter of waiting the for next dramatic event to unfold.

It was in the early hours of the following morning that we discovered what this might entail. As the skies trembled with the roar of some 250 to 300 heavy bombers flying above us another fear suddenly gripped us. As these overhead planes flew north an almighty barrage of enemy shells was unleashed from somewhere inland. We later realised that the centre of this barrage was near Monte Casino. Some of our veteran soldiers believed that it's intensity compared with the fire-power discharged in the Desert Conflict at El Alemein.

During the next six days we became encouraged by a series of reports of Allied progress that we heard. On 13th. May, the Allies had pushed on notably. In the next two days similar attacks had been made on each front across Italy. On 16th. came news that gains had been made on two fronts – the Gustav Line and the Adolph Hitler Winter Line – which had both been obstructive for months before.

The next day the Germans were even dislodged from their positions in the Monte Cassino region. Bitter fighting between our enemy and the Polish Fifth Rnesowa Division resulted in the dislodgement of the former. Whilst the Poles held their newly acquired ground in the face of fierce counter-attacks the British also played a significant role too. From the south, units of the British Infantry virtually surrounded the city. Once they had driven forcefully across Highway Six they were able to rebuff all attempts to re-capture the road. The following day the Eighteenth Carpathian Division stormed into the region and in the early afternoon four Divisions of Ten Brigade captured Cassino. This was a huge morale-boosting success for the Allied forces.

This turning point meant that a 'Roman Holiday' in the making was definitely possible in the near future for my colleagues and I! We realised that first we would probably have to engage the enemy again and continue to struggle like Titans to overcome his resistance. Little by little we began to win the upper hand. On 19th May Esperia was taken by the Allies as some 400 of our bomber aeroplanes moved towards the fringes of the Hitler Line.

The weather still held little or no respect for our successes. On 20th. the heavens still deluged our positions with excessive rainfall. With the delight of hearing that Gaeta had also been taken I flung an old pair of boots over the cliff edge near our

Warship firing into enemy positions N of Beachhead

dug-outs. Within seconds I was reminded of the rashness of my careless behaviour when a loud explosion indicated I had set off a mine with my flying footwear!

Innumerable waves of bomber planes continued to fly over our position. Some were directed towards Cisterna on 22nd. May. On the same day our Fifth Division was ordered to mount a diversionary attack. It fell to our Fifth Division to hold Anzio against the attempts of the German Fourth Parachute Division's attack. From time to time we could clearly hear the scream of shells from one of the Royal Navy's large cruisers attempting to pound the enemy's position. On the following day it was the turn or the American cruisers to fire broadside after broadside in the same direction.

By the 25th. May we believed that the enemy at Cisterna had been surrounded and the Germans began to pull out of the Anzio beachhead district. The effectiveness of our efforts against the Germans was such that on this day the main Fifth Army units from Cassino were able to join with the Anzio units in a combined sweep towards Rome.

When Littoria was taken in the surge of 26th, we managed to enjoy a slight rest from our demanding work. We attended a mobile cinema show on that day to see 'Hold that Ghost'. Some amongst us could not help comparing our wan and pale looks also – enhanced by the demands of the three previous months – to those of ghosts and skeletons.

The sounds and sights of death were always close to us as May drew to a close in 1944. Our naval bombardments were such that the ship's gun barrels must have been 'red hot' with their continuous exertions. Even the most reliable of units in our ranks – such as the Royal Engineers – were beginning to feel the 'pace' of insatiable demands on them. On 28th., for example, we heard that one of our jeeps on the 'cleared' route to Rome had been destroyed by an undetected mine. Anzio Annie was also still hurtling its huge shells towards our positions. Fortunately it was captured soon afterwards by our own troops. Perhaps the nearest each of the men in my unit came to death was on 29th. May when Cecil, our fitter was hit in the arm by a sniper. I gave him first-aid before I was able to ask the medics for their help.

Despite such omnipresent dangers we began, little by little, to feel a new wave of expectancy slowly creeping through our ranks. Never in our wildest dreams, however, did we realise that in the month of June in that year our efforts would be indelibly stamped as irreversibly victorious in the annals of military history. It was almost in disbelief that we were later to realise just how important our progress in this month been. At the same time despite our remarkable achievements our successes were to be somewhat overshadowed by the momentous invasion mounted by the Allied forces upon France's Normandy beaches on D.Day, 6th June. This was the European theatre of war which most captured the minds and imagination of those who hoped to see a truly historical blow against our enemy.

Meanwhile our efforts in Italy continued to pay huge dividends. On 1st. of that month the Allies struck hard at Valmontone and its adjacent areas. Though the Germans resisted heroically there it was eventually taken the following day. This in turn allowed the free powers to 'fan out' their troops to take Palestrina, Cave and Labico within the next two days.

Throughout this offensive movement the Allied forces naval units were actively supporting these land operations. We were especially appreciative of their efforts in patrolling the coastal areas, their protection of the supply lines to Anzio itself and their delivery of shell fire support to the main front and left flank of the beachhead itself. On the land the Fifth Division beat off a heavy counter-attack and was able to advance further along the coast. Such was the success of all involved that by 6pm. on the 2nd. June Allied forces were fifteen miles away from Rome.

The following day the heavy armed pressure was so intense that our forces had advanced a further eight miles towards the capital city. At 7am. the next day a special bulletin announced that the Fifth Army and the Fifth Division had reached the outskirts themselves. We, in the British sector of the advance, were then instructed to keep static our position on the outskirts. On the 5th. June 1944 our high command decided that the American forces should be the first to enter the Eternal City. One 'stray' aircraft did drop a stick of four bombs within fifty yards of us but that was the only opposition we confronted on that historic day. Fortunately little damage was incurred by us.

We were thus able to move with little discomfort to a fresh staging post to the south west of Rome. We travelled along a coastal road to the historic shores outside Ostia some eight miles to the west of the capital. As we settled in at our sandy seaside site we eagerly listened to a report, at 6pm. that evening, to details of the Allied forces invasion in France. Despite the heroic struggles of both the Allied forces and those of their foe on this War Front in Italy it was the invasion of France that was destined to become the most famous.

The rest of our time spent in or near the Italian capital city in June was to be quite unforgettable. The next ten days my colleagues and I experienced all the those feelings brought on by a mixed cocktail of emotions. The fruits of freedom, the heady

Rome from the top of St. Peters 2 days after fall

sense of success, the mundane duties of army life and the experience of being near death and close to serious injury all seemed to affect us.

Whilst other units had to press onwards beyond Rome, however, ours was fortunate to be able to take our recovery truck and head into the City itself on 8th. June. The next day I was fortunate to go with an official party consisting of mixed ranks from our three main services, to attend an audience with his Holiness, Pope Pious X1, in the Square of St. Peter. From 11th. to 15th. I had the added good fortune to make a series of further visits to see many of the City's most famous monuments. These included the Coliseum, the Victor Emmanuel Monument and the Royal Opera House.

Having enjoyed such unforgettable opportunities to savour the historic delights of that remarkable city I was somewhat reluctant to leave the district. On 15th. June, nevertheless, we moved on towards Capua in the south. We journeyed some 125

King Victor Emanuel memorial

miles, via Anzio, Nettuno, Terracina and Formia, to the Garigliano region. At 12.30am. we arrived at our campsite for a stay that lasted three days. It was somewhat with a sense of nostalgia that I reflected there on my latest trip through Anzio. I was struck by the peace and tranquillity of that district at that time and could not but be moved when I recalled the sheer hell that had been experienced by the numerous, brave soldiers who fought to capture and retain it.

Before leaving Capua by rail., at 8am. of 19th June, we had regained some of the normality of the non-combative role of army life. I was grateful, for example, to be given the opportunity in camp to see dear old George Formby in the film 'Bell-Bottom George'. Such entertainment gave us the chance to reflect once more on the prospects of civilian life. Our train journey from Capua to the seaport of Naples lasted about two hours . When we eventually marched through the docks therein I could not help but spare a thought or two for my family and friends back in my home port of Liverpool. I soon found that the SS Ascania, boarded by us in Naples, however, was bound for Egypt on 20th. June. Once again it was a case of sailing off 'into the unknown'. By this time I was able to be thankful for my good health and the fact that I had not been seriously injured to-date. Many of my

fellow army comrades had not been so fortunate during those
dire months of our historic march through Italy.

'Y' Div Sgt writing home after fall of Rome Aug 1943

Chapter Nine

The Holy Land and Heavenly Music, 1944.

Having been at the centre of such a remarkable victory as the 'winning of Rome' from the enemy I could not help but wonder if we would be rewarded by those who commanded us. This was not to be so because, as we later realised the success had been just one major step in a necessary series of 'giant strides' that had to be made. If the 'spoils' did not fall to us as victors we certainly felt our 'grand tour' in the Mediterranean and Near East was unique. In peace time such travel as we had undertaken could only have been financed by the extremely wealthy or privileged. For someone like myself who until 1939 'strayed' little from the environs of Liverpool, this formed a major part of my 'journey of a life time'.

On 21st. June 1944 our troopships docked in Valetta on the island of Malta, and we wondered if we would be allowed shore 'leave'. When we misunderstood a message from our ship's inter-communications system many of us actually did disembark. The moment we returned at 23,00 hours we were given a verbal 'dressing down' because only the ship's crew – and not 'all hands' – had been granted leave!

In keeping with our customary early morning starts we sailed out from Malta at 7am. on 22nd. Some three and one hours 'out' we were joined by yet another convoy of ships that included such well-known vessels as the Britannic and the Duchess of Bedford. Three days later we arrived in the Egyptian port of Alexandria at 8am. Our arrival was greeted with an air-raid alarm, so we had to stay aboard all day. Yet again we realised that there was still no 'escape' from the war for us. Fortunately, with no damage incurred, the 'All-Clear', at 11.40am., was welcomed by us.

When we finally did leave the ship, for a new land base, it was at 6.15pm. the next-day. We dashed to catch the 8.00pm. train to Cairo. Our destination and 'holiday home' on this occasion was to be the Ben Youseff Camp. Here, even at our arrival time at 7.00am on 26th it was extremely hot. Two days later we were assigned a series of 'new' vehicles and we were ordered to keep them ready for immediate use. Despite this order a small contingent from amongst us managed to secure a liberty pass for a short period.

About this time I was instructed to assist those who were assigned camp night-time guard duty. My 'reward' for this was a chance to see the film 'Journey for Margaret' at the camp cinema during the next-day. The theme chanced to be about the Second World War. In the film an American newspaper correspondent brought a London Blitz orphan to his home in the U.S.A. A young Margaret O'Brien and Robert Young played the key parts in this touching melodrama that was probably deliberately produced to enlist support in the United States for the 'besieged' Londoners at that time of the 'blitz'.

My own thoughts about the United Kingdom focused northwards – on Liverpool – on 1st. July. This was the date of my birthday. Although there was no party, cake or candles to celebrate with I did, almost miraculously, receive a birthday card. To me this had a charmed aura about it for I had convinced myself that my family may have given up hope of reaching me with messages. How touching it was to read this single piece of mail signed by my mother and other members of my family. Their wish of 'hope you will be home soon' was deeply touching

On 6th. July we had to move on to another base - yet again! Having filled our petrol tanks at 7am. we travelled 110m miles and arrived at Ismalia at 6 o'clock in the evening. This was but the first stage in a further desert travel saga because on the following day we left our camp at Ismalia, crossed the Suez Canal and then undertook a long trek through the Sinia Desert. To help reduce the bright glare from the hot, burning sun we were issued with green-lensed sun glasses. By the time we reached our next desert

Ben Yousef near Cairo   *L.A.D. in Sini Desert*   *Stores Lorry Sini*

camp, at approximately 8.30pm. we had travelled another 178miles.

The following day our journey to reach Nathania was somewhat shorter – just 110miles for this stage. Leaving at 6.30am. we were able to reach our destination by 2pm. We were not able to rest once we had reached our goal, however, for we had yet to undertake the routine maintenance of our vehicles. Our chief problems arose as before from the omnipresent particles of sand that crept into the carburettors, dynamos, regulators and the starter-motors. Nevertheless I did manage to 'escape' on leave and journeyed into nearby Nathanya to have my photographs processed. Together with several colleagues I was able to enjoy the chance to swim at a nearby beach. How much clearer and warmer the water was than my native River Mersey.

On 18th July I and three others decided to continue our 'holiday' activities by taking a taxi into the Holy City of Jerusalem. This was regarded as a unique privilege by each of us. Once more we felt we had stumbled by chance upon the opportunity of a life-time. Our taxi driver acted as a guide and drove us to both Ascension Hill – revered as the site of Christ's return to his heavenly father – and then we went on to Bethlehem. To visit the latter, the birth place of the Saviour, was extremely comforting and gave us time to reflect in prayer on the

Jerusalem and Bethlehem

need for peace in our war-torn world. We felt overjoyed by the visits to the Church that stood where Jesus had reputedly been born. The atmosphere within the Church was uniquely moving for each of us.

The urge to pray in this holy place brought vividly to mind those nightly prayers of thanksgiving I had made throughout my career in the army. Often before retiring I had whispered a prayer to God in thanks for keeping me safe particularly after the mayhem and carnage of battle. My prayers also included pleas for the safety and well-being of my family and friends. The poignant visit to this reassuring shrine was one that I held dear throughout the rest of the war.

The following morning we jumped at the chance to travel into Jericho and then swim or 'float' in the extreme buoyancy of the Dead Sea waters. At lunch time we returned to Jerusalem for a meal near the Church of the Twelve Nations. This unusual building had twelve domes in honour of these nations. To complete a most satisfactory day we attended a mobile cinema show to see the Metro Golwyn Mayer film entitled 'Mrs. Miniver'. Yet again this was a performance that had a poignant Second World War theme. It's cast included Greer Garson, Walter Pidgeon and Dame May Whitty. The final stage of our Holy Land tour occurred on July 20th. when we managed to reach Mount Calvary, the hilly site where Christ had been crucified.

This period of leave came to an end on the following day when

Church of the Twelve Nations and Church of Nativity

I and my colleagues left Nathanya at 3pm. to travel to Tel Aviv. Fortunately this was a short trip and at 4pm., when we arrived at the city, we received instructions to prepare for an Armament Artificers course in Egypt. This was a course specifically designed to improve the skills of those such as myself who previously worked as electrical and mechanical personnel in the Base or other small units such as the L.A.D.

This new training venture necessitated my packing all my belongings and moving to Egypt. With my kit bag, valise, a small pack and my rifle I began my return journey to that ancient country. In all this meant I had to travel some 320 miles with only an overnight stop at Ez-Luge before reaching my destination at Tel-El-Kebir. My 'reward' for my endeavour was received on 24th. July when I began the course for promotion to the rank of staff-sergeant. As soon as I began the course I was given an initial promotion to the rank of sergeant.

Strangely, even after all my travels, I had always been a little nervous when I had to confront a new and demanding situation. My reaction to the preliminary test papers – in Mathematics, that included 'Mensuration' and Geometry – on 25th. July 1944 was far more extreme than I expected. I had not been engaged on the course for more than a few days when one night I reacted forcibly to the contraction of dysentery! By 7th. August I was admitted to hospital still suffering from the dreaded 'galloping wild' symptoms of the illness. Being permitted no solid food I was allowed only fluids and the issue of Sulphaguanadine four times each day. Although I was eventually discharged from the hospital on 16th. of the month I continued my course of treatment. By this time I felt a little more able to receive the well-intentioned jibes of my colleagues – some inferring it was the 'Mummies Curse' or Egypt's version of the 'Pharaohs Revenge'.

As somewhat unmerciful employers my senior officers sent me back to continue on my course – the electrical one that is and not the one to prevent other more personal and more painful discharges of energy! On 18th. I took my final test paper though still feeling somewhat groggy. The next day whilst at the base depot at 5pm. I heard I had received a 'pass' grade.

Once again my gipys-like life caused me to 'move onwards'. On 20th of that month I received orders to join the 338 Workshop Company for 'general electrical duties'. It was not until the 9th. September that I actually left the Tel-EK camp. A truck journey to the nearest railway station allowed me to take a train to Port Said. At 2pm., in intense heat, I boarded the SS Monarch of Bermuda. I must admit that by this time I felt more like a monarch's messenger than a 'king'. On 10th. at 5pm. in the company of many other ranked and non-ranked army personnel we set sail. The comparatively comfortable facilities aboard the vessel were much appreciated. It was with considerable gratitude that I joined the large cinema show audience in the ship's lounge. The world famous Abbot and Costello film star comedy team starred in the film we watched. Afterwards it was a delight to join the boisterous outburst of community singing when many of the male ranks mimicked the voices of lady singers and were greeted by a burst of spontaneous laughter and applause for their efforts.

On 12th. of that month, as the sea began to swell noticeably, our clocks were 'put back' one hour in time. This was done to coincide with international time zone demands. With six ships in total in our convoy and some 4,700 personnel aboard ours it was considerably large number of bodies for the senior officers to be responsible for. Although light-hearted antics by some amongst us were tolerated, a good standard of discipline was therefore always essential. Morale, too, was generally raised by organised periods of relaxation, like the showing of the film 'Charlie's American Aunt' as we sailed through the Gulf of Taranto. This viewing was fully appreciated by most. The chance to see such well known stars as Jack Benny, Kay Francis, Anne Baxter and Edmund Gwenn, was readily seized upon. These personalities, on this occasion, were involved in a plot where an Oxford undergraduate had to impersonate his own aunt from Brazil. Their performances were so professional that their humorous antics appealed to most in our multi-international audience and met with thunderous applause at the conclusion of the film.

On 15th. September our vessel entered Italian waters and docked in Taranto at 11.30am. When we eventually disembarked we headed for our 'new' base camp and arrived there about 2.30pm. To remind us that we were not on holiday we went on a four mile 'route-march exercise' after a late lunch. Sleeping in tents as we did and regularly rising at dawn throughout the next week we quickly realised again that British army life was structured within a very strict code of discipline. Sometimes our routines were changed. This happened on 17th. when we washed our clothes after an early breakfast. Unlike my mother 'back home' we used buckets to dunk our clothes in. Our water was primarily taken from water carts and on occasions straight from a local river! In the evening we were also invited to attend an unusually sited army 'cinema show'. On this occasion it was held in a stone quarry and the main film was aptly entitled 'Five Graves to Cairo'? When I and many of my colleagues recalled our dysentery-induced, 'wild gallops' to the latrines in Egypt we could not but help joke with one another how, but for our courses of Sulphaguanadine there might well have been an additional one thousand and five graves in Cairo!

The film itself was in truth a marvellous one made by Paramount Pictures Incorporated. It was something of a pipe-dream plot – with British spies attempting to destroy the Germans secret ammunition supply 'dumps' of Field Marshall Rommel. Though the main theme had been, I considered, hastily written and based on the first major Second World War success of the British Army, the actors performances were, nevertheless superb. Those by Franchot Tone, Anne Baxter, Eric Von Stronheim and Akin Tamiroff were particularly memorable. Yet again they not only glamorised our role in the North African Campaign but permitted us to relax for a few hours in an imagined world of romance and intrigue.

It was because it was generally too exhausting for us to carry out strenuous activities in the heat of the day that we usually 'worked' each morning and relaxed after midday. Thus it was on 19th. that after lunch some of us took a 'liberty truck' to the railway station at Bagni Chiantona. This small town with its popular beach was about twelve miles to the West of Taranto. At the former we enjoyed the opportunities to swim and make use of a cafe' nearby. Here, too, we were able to use our cameras to take photographs that we were able to send 'home'. Though we returned to camp that evening, we went back to Chiatona after rifle practice the following morning. On the third consecutive day we again we were able to return to our beach relaxation location but, since there were no trains on 22nd. September, we walked instead. In the extreme heat at that time our seven mile journey took us about two hours on foot.

This spell of 'fitness training' continued on the following day when we undertook a session of army physical exercises and rifle drill. As something of a change of relaxation pursuits that afternoon a large contingent of us visited the Littoria Theatre for an especially organised Italian film show. The 'live' performance was basically one of operatic and orchestral music. Though it was initially regarded by some as mainly for those who were lovers of classical music it was fully appreciated by most, if not all, of those fortunate enough to attend.

It was sometime during those visits to the beach, the cinema and the classical music performance that my inner tension at having been so close to death at Anzio began to lessen, little by little. I did not know at this particular point in time that I would never in the future come so perilously close to the enemy's live shells, bullets and other deadly weapons of war as I had at that terrifying beach-head. Though our forces were still heavily engaged on several European fronts I was never to be ordered again into front line, battle-field action. This was a decision about my life and well being that I had no control over.

It was only when the war was over that I was able to fully realise the life threatening dangers that my brothers-in-arms and I had been forced to face. For the time being I was still far away from home and became determined to accept any small comforts I might find there. Since I was an admirer of the Italian classical music achievements I determined at that point to seize any opportunity – like the concert above – to attend any concert that might 'come my way'. In this modern era of unprecedented man-made destruction and havoc it was something that I believed might help to pull me through the ordeals of war. I felt sure at that point that others around me would also be holding dear to themselves the light of a similar hope.

British Soldiers!

You are fighting and dying far away from your country while the Yanks are putting up their tents in Merry Old England. They've got lots of money and loads of time to chase after your women.

And what about you?

THE BEACH-HEAD

is going to be the big blow against the Germans.

Wasn't that the slogan when the Allied troops landed at Nettuno on January 21st?

TODAY

exactly three months of hard fighting have passed and you can now celebrate this event. But it is still merely a beach-head, paved with the skulls of thousands of British and American soldiers!

The Beach-Head has become a Death's Head!

It is welcoming You with a grin, and also those who are coming after you across the sea for an appointment with death.

Do they know what they are in for?
Yes, they feel that they are landing on a

DEATH'S HEAD

A I - 065 4-44

Two more leaflets dropped by Germans

Chapter Ten

Music, Maestro Please, 1944-45

As I waited at the railway station near Taranto base, on the 25th. September 1944, the words and melodies of several popular songs came into my mind. This was but one of many quizzes that I used to help 'while away the time' as I waited in numerous queues throughout my life in the army. Whilst at the station we endured a torrential cloudburst. 'Singing in the Rain' was one well-known tune that I sang to myself as being most appropriate at that point in time.

In total my comrades and I had a six hour wait before a train finally arrived at 7pm. This Chattanooga Choo Choo took us, by chance, along the track we had used on a walking tour to the beach a few days earlier. It was to be a rail journey that lasted throughout the hours of darkness. It became apparent from time to time, as we travelled, that we had to cross a series of rivers and had to enter a number of long tunnels. These, I was informed later led under the Southern Alps. Whenever we were able to discern any features we were impressed by the land-scape scenes visible from the Alpine ridges that our train sped across. The ever changing picturesque sights finally terminated about 8am. the following morning when we stopped for 'breakfast' at Salerno.

After a most welcome meal we continued on our journey until we reached the Central Railway Station at Naples. Prior to our arrival we were able to catch a glimpse of the remarkable ruins of the Roman City site at Pompeii. Our tourist 'status' was finally brought to an end, at 11am., when we were directed from the train and ordered to make our way towards the army trucks waiting to take our contingent to new billets. These quarters were in a former factory building some five miles to the south of the great seaport of Naples.

On this occasion we did not have far to 'walk to work' because opposite our new place of residence was the 16th. Base of the workshops of the R.E.M.E. It was shortly after settling into our latest home that we reported to the workshop for details of our duties. I was instructed to join F section to share the repair and maintenance work on the tanks, the armoured cars, the quads and some of the artillery's weapons. These in turn were to be sent for use in Northern Italy and France.

When we were eventually given our first evening 'liberty' pass I joined a large group of comrades heading for 'the Palace'. This was neither a royal residence nor a house of ill-repute but simply the local NAAFI base. Many of us were made to feel like 'royalty' when we went within its noble walls. Once inside we were able to use our British military currency to buy anything from a mug of tea to a full, home style meal.

Lunch at Royal Palace

It was the opportunity to visit British facilities such as the NAAFI which helped to substitute several facets of our much missed 'Pommie' style of life. Without fully realising this during our long years of absence from home, it helped to keep our spirits high. These were testing times away from the people and places so dear to us. Even as 'veterans' or battle-weary soldiers I am sure most of us silently nurtured the hope of seeing our loved ones as soon as possible. It was very much the case of absence making the heart grow fonder after being such a long time away from them.

Following on from the swamp-like conditions and the constant combat and battle-alertness we had experienced over several months at Anzio we were now more than ready to settle into the relative carefreeness of British-style, 'colonial life' abroad. During the ensuing months it was pleasant for me to follow a pattern of maintaining army vehicles in the cool of each day and then being

Royal Palace, Naples

given regular leave periods to sample the attractive forms of cultured entertainment in nearby Naples.

On most days of the week, including weekends there were orchestral concerts in the State Rooms of the Royal Palace in the city. Sometimes these celebrations were conducted on a large balcony facade overlooking the Bay of Naples itself. Especially popular with many of our troops were those operatic arias performed by both male and female artists of outstanding talent at the San Carlo Opera House.

My regular sojourns to the San Carlo Opera House helped me, for several hours at a time, to transcend many of the anxieties of a bitterly war-torn world. At the same time these visits occasionally induced something of an emotional turmoil within me for they transported me back in time through the musical memories I had so vividly retained of the times in the 1930's which I had enjoyed with my father.

One recollection of those distant days I recalled was how I had entered the musical emporium of Smith's Shop, in Liverpool's

Lord Street, in 1931. That had been the occasion when we went to purchase our very first 'radio gramophone'. The demonstration record at this time had been that of Beniamino Gigli singing 'The Geldia Manina', from La Boheme. How touching it was when I went to see him and hear him live in the San Carlo – the second most renowned House of Opera in Italy.

It was on the 22nd. October I undertook my first visit to the San Carlo. The first production I enjoyed here was entitled Lucia de Lammermore. Though a seat in the stalls was relatively cheap – about five pence in modern value – it was the high quality of the performances and not the low entrance charge that attracted capacity audiences!

On each of my visits I believe about ninety per cent of the audience was drawn from the Armed services. With so many famous performers regularly singing there – they included Gigli's daughter Rina, Tagliavini, Tito Gobbi, Mariano Caruso, Maria Pedrini, Benuvento Franci and conductor Franco Patane – it became something of a musical shrine for many Service visitors. Indeed I am given to understand that a special plaque in the foyer of the Opera House now commemorates the war-time popularity of those concerts with allied service personnel.

One particular visit brought a surprise for me that neither my father nor I could ever even in our wildest dreams have dreamed of . Having been delighted on many occasions by the quality of the San Carlo productions – these included La Traviata, Carmen, Andrea Chenier, Cav and Pag – I succeeded on one occasion in obtaining a seat for Puccini's La Boheme. This included an unforgettable performance by Gigli himself.

Afterwards, by sheer chance, I was able to approach this supreme artist whom many regarded as the tenor most correctly recognised as Caruso's operatic successor. When I came close to him I managed to attract his attention and he was kind enough to respond to me, if only for a few seconds, and in somewhat broken English.

Undoubtedly, the Opera House had a charismatic charm for

many of the men from the armed services who visited it so frequently. For me it became a welcome release from both the haunting memories of the battlefront zones and from the everyday maintenance and repair duties carried out at the 16th Base Workshops.

It was after one such visit, sometime between the 30th September 1944 and the 11th October, that I had been assigned at my base to do work on some 150 armoured cars. During this period of specialised duties I was also transferred from time to time to carry out some modifications on both Sherman and Churchill tanks. To help 'fine tune' the skills of my colleagues and myself a number of us had to attend a series of courses that extended throughout the Winter months. Whenever any work of this nature was completed it was carefully scrutinised by members of the resident inspectorate body that was attached to our base.

It was not 'all work and no play' however for whenever an off-duty period came my way I would join with other colleagues

Royal Palace (NAFFI). Cinema

to take a liberty truck to the San Carlo, to a cinema or simply to do some shopping.

By chance, my second favourite source of entertainment stood adjacent to the San Carlo Opera House. Here there was an ornately decorated building which housed a cinema. This had a most beautifully decorated interior. One film of note that I enjoyed there was entitled 'This Happy Breed'. Directed by David Lean, the theme of this I clearly remember was that of London family life between the two Great Wars. When I went to see it, the 'show' lasted two hours. The cast, which included Robert Newton, Stanley Holloway, John Mills and Kay Walsh, kept the audience entranced.

On other occasions I set off to do some shopping in the very popular Via Roma district of Naples. Here were many fine establishments selling jewellery, books and other souvenirs. It was an additional treat for many of us to 'stop off' at the welcoming and cheerful Salvation Army canteen in this shopping precinct.

That is not to say that day to day army life at our base was always tedious. Whenever possible my colleagues and I would try to keep our spirits high by resorting to the telling of humorous anecdotes and by indulging in comic deceits aimed at 'raising' a laugh. One such scene was played out in the Summer of 1945 with myself as the intended 'stooge'. It occurred one day as I was engaged in the workshop bay in correcting the internal mechanical problems of a Churchill tank. I was suddenly startled when the administrative sergeant appeared from nowhere and shouted loudly that a new man had been assigned to us and that I was to 'show him the ropes'. Within a few moments of conversation with the 'freshman' I realised that he and I only lived about five hundred yards from each other in 'dear old Liverpool Town'. As we engaged in rapid, light-hearted banter in which we compared local place names and personalities, it became apparent that our 'beloved' administrative sergeant must have had a sense of humour equal to that which Scousers or Liverpudlians, were well-known for. Though I had met quite a

Author with his brother Raymond

number of Liverpool lads on my epic journey this latest acquaintance, one Ronnie Cosgrove lived closest to my home.

A further chance meeting with a fellow Liverpool exile was to recur on the 3rd. July in that year. This second occasion, however, was to be even more remarkable than the former. I had just entered my billet after my afternoon's work when I became dumbstruck with the familiar face I recognised. There standing in front of me was my brother Raymond.

It transpired that fate had brought him into Naples because he was a merchant seaman serving aboard the SS Ascania, a troop-carrying vessel. He had shown outstanding resolve to find me because he had initially known little apart from the fact that my base was situated some three or four miles outside the port of Naples. The strength of his single-minded attitude to life became more and more apparent during our celebratory drinking session at the Palace NAFFI, as he began to recount some of the dangers he had confronted whilst at sea.

Little by little he began to reveal some of the terrifying experiences he and his shipmates had been subjected to when threatened by both the German U-boats and aircraft.

One of these incidents had occurred whilst he was serving aboard the Queen Mary on the 2nd. October, 1942. It appeared that this giant-sized ship of the Cunard Line inadvertently ploughed into the cruiser HMS Curacao at 2.10pm. and the latter sank very quickly. Raymond revealed that the 'Mary' was travelling at about twenty eight and a half knots at the moment of impact. He remembered feeling how that grand vessel shuddered a little as a result of the collision but it was not permitted to stop for any survivors since she was carrying about 15,000 American troops. These lives and the mighty ship herself would have been placed in acute danger if she had mounted a search-and, rescue operation. As a direct consequence of the collision the Curacao and some 331 persons aboard her were drowned.

When I discovered that Raymond was shortly to leave Naples I made a dash and gathered some presents for both my mother and sister. He accepted these and promised to do his best to deliver them safely. It was only when he had left that I realised how close our paths were to coinciding in 1942. My voyage from Scotland to South Africa had occurred just seven months before the Queen Mary's fateful ramming of the unfortunate Curacao. I shivered when I realised how lucky our vessel had been when compared to the Curacao as we had taken the same route.

My good fortune in October 1945 was to carry on into November of that year. I did not know it at the time but again fate was beginning to unfold a series of events that would become indelibly written into my memory.

Yet again the boundless courage, deep determination and unremitting selflessness of a member of the 'Show Biz' fraternity was to amaze many of my colleagues and myself. We as soldiers had seen innumerable acts of valour, heroism and devotion to duty on the blood-soaked fields of battle that lay behind us. To see comparable risks of life and limb being undertaken by our civilian entertainers was both touching and singularly uplifting.

This additional exciting chapter during my military service began when I heard that the famous film star Gracie Fields had returned to Italy to take up residence just beyond Naples, on the Isle of Capri. As more news filtered through it became known that among her first professional engagements would be a special appearance at the San Carlo Opera House for a Remembrance Day Service. After this she would immediately travel to the nearby Bellini Theatre for an extended 'live' performance for the armed services personnel.

Even the most uninformed listeners to radio amongst the

11- 11- 45

PROGRAMME

.... PROGRAMME ....

A SPECIAL REMEMBRANCE DAY PROGRAMME

THE S. CARLO OPERA HOUSE ORCHESTRA

Conducted by: U G O   R A P A L O

with GRACIE FIELDS

and

THE BAND OF THE ROYAL ULSTER RIFLES

1. Symphonic Poem « On the Trail »   FERDE GROFÉ

2. Symphonic Poem

   « The Night Procession »   RABAUD

3. Overture « I Vespri Siciliani »   VERDI

   Interval 15 mins.

4. Overture 1812   TCHAIKOWSKI

5. Enigma Variations   ELGAR
   a) Variation No. 12
   b) Variation No. 9

6. GRACIE FIELDS
   « Land of Hope and Glory »

7. LESSON - Revelations. Chap. 7 - Verses 9-17
   PRAYERS
   Last Post   Reveille.
   « ABIDE WITH ME. »

Smoking is not permitted in the Auditorium or in the first, second or third floor corridors

Remembrance day Programme San Carlo.

troops had a sentimental regard for this Lancashire comedienne / film actress. As a fervent cinema buff I was only too happy to recall for 'the lads' the names and dates of the films she had made up to this point in the war. During the economic depression in the Thirties she had been able to lift the gloom from the lives of many ordinary working men and women in Britain. Her films, which included 'Sally in Our Ally', 1931, 'Sing as We Go'. 1934, 'Queen of Hearts', 1936 and 'Shipyard Sally' in 1940, had been among my favourites. How the word spread like wild fire throughout our ranks that during the Special Service on the 11th. November 1945 she would sing 'Land of Hope and Glory'.

As soon as these details became known the management at the San Carlo was inundated with applications for tickets for seats at the theatre. Though all seats were 'sold out' within hours of tickets becoming available I counted myself fortunate enough to be able to obtain one. The growing intensity of the excited reaction must have reached Gracie quickly for we soon heard how she was also feeling singularly moved at the prospect of singing before so many of her countrymen on such a solemn occasion. Like the thorough professional she was she undertook to rigorously practise her singing whilst at home in her villa on the Isle of Capri. At the same time the Band of the Royal Ulster Rifles, which was to accompany her, was diligently rehearsing at the San Carlo itself.

Though she had intended to cross the Bay of Naples by boat on Saturday her plans to reach the seaport from her island home on Capri were unavoidably disrupted. During the course of the day the weather conditions became appalling. Such were the dangers to shipping in the Bay it was regarded as being impossible for any vessel to leave the Isle of Capri.

Signals between ENSA and the Allied Forces Headquarters at Naples were frequently exchanged as anxiety increased about Gracie being able to fulfil her planned musical engagements. Though the great lady herself was eager to come across that tempestuous stretch of Sea, the Sea itself was not eager to permit her to do so. For her part she consoled everyone involved telling them "not to worry". Some way or other, she determined, she would make the crossing.

On the Sunday morning, the day of the performance, the position became more grim. Each report from the Royal Navy indicated that such a crossing as Gracie planned was impossible. Meanwhile at the San Carlo in Naples, ENSA were reviewing the situation with alarm. Plans made to the Royal Navy and the R.A.F. to send out an aeroplane to assist were ruled out because at that time there was no suitable landing place on Capri.

As time ticked by Gracie herself was reported to be most upset because she had never let down any audience before. "We're all going crazy over here" she admitted as she heard yet another report that the sea route was absolutely impossible. A further hour passed as permission was even sought to get a 'crash boat' to assist with her passage. The Royal Navy it seemed was doing everything within their power to help her to honour her commitment.

As the crowds gathered and the long queues of admirers stretched outside the San Carlo some people even believed Gracie had already reached the theatre. Plans, however, had to be drawn up behind the scenes, to cater for the eventuality of Gracie being unable to begin her concert by 8.30pm. Major Lines of 56 Area gave instructions that if she had not attended for the Armistice Concert and Service by the above time an announcement would be broadcast about her circumstances. In that event the Royal Ulster Rifles Band would begin to play 'Land of Hope and Glory' and this would be followed by Armistice Prayers – to be conducted by the Armed Forces Chaplains present.

Even when the vast audience had taken its seats and filled the theatre most still believed that Gracie would appear as indicated in the programmes. All those 'back-stage' despaired at this point that she would ever be able to appear. The 8.30pm deadline came but by a stroke of good fortune the San Carlos orchestra was still playing its rendition of the lengthy Enigma Variations.

When the work was completed the conductor began to prepare his musicians for their next item but a tremendous commotion was clearly audible from behind the theatre's main stage. Those personnel backstage were heartened by the arrival of a panting and gasping Gunner Blackburn R. A. who dashed up the stairs to the stage to blurt out 'She's here!'

Sure enough she was but in a most pitiable state. She had dragged herself up the stairs, looking somewhat white-faced, ill and haggard. Gracie was helped into her dressing room by her husband Monty Banks, Major Ridgeway and her pianist Frank Bunn.

How had the miraculous passage in such violent conditions been achieved? It appears that the Royal Navy had sent out a motorised launch and at 6pm. had managed to reach Capri. One hour later with Gracie aboard it made a 'nightmare crossing' to return to Naples by 8.22pm.

Many experienced seamen pronounced Gracie would have been perfectly correct to have refused to travel in such threatening conditions. It transpired that such was her resolve to make the crossing that she actually uttered a prayer of thanksgiving when the motor launch first came into view at Capri. Though the journey could not have been worse her one determined thought was that 'the show must go on'.

Nevertheless when she finally arrived at the San Carlo and dragged herself doggedly up the back stairs many who witnessed her bedraggled state believed she would be unable to perform on stage. She did so even though several onlookers backstage must have wondered how she managed it. It was only ten minutes after she arrived in a state of near collapse that she was singing 'Land of Hope and Glory' with all the 'fire' and spirit she was renowned for.

After this first rendition the orchestra, audience, and stage hands, rose as one to greet her performance with rousing applause. Her stamina and single-mindedness had helped her to determine at this point that the audience was truly deserving of being given 'value for money'. Nobody anticipated that she would extend her performance at this point in time.

Though still on stage at 9pm. she had been due to perform at the Bellini theatre at the same time. It would appear that the packed audience at the latter had been awaiting her appearance for more than an hour. Despite appeals from those trying to attract her attention in the San Carlo's wings she continued with her repertoire of jokes, a further song and then finally she sang her much admired version of 'The Lord's Prayer'. The audience at the San Carlo had not been promised an extended performance by Gracie but they gratefully accepted this wonderful gift from her. Their memorable ovation when she finally concluded her act seemed both thunderous and interminable.

How she managed to stand on that stage and entertain so completely as she did – after her perilous journey to the theatre – baffled even the most battle-hardened veterans. She was virtually carried in a state of collapse to her dressing room when she came off stage. We had much to wonder at as the programme concluded nostalgically with 'The Last Post' and then the hymn 'Abide with Me'.

Outside the theatre, at 9.15pm., Gracie was surrounded by those officers responsible for her safety. She was guided to an awaiting motorcar which was preceded by a military police-driven jeep. At breakneck speed both these vehicles sped down the Via Roma and reached the Bellini in little more than a few minutes.

By this time Gracie herself was almost speechless but she managed to respond with her normal enthusiasm to the huge throngs of servicemen outside the theatre. Although they had been unable to obtain tickets for her performance they released spontaneous cheers of appreciation as she emerged from her vehicle. As she was assisted up the forty steps of the staircase leading to her dressing room she began again the same, almost frenzied preparations for her appearance at the Bellini as she had undertaken at the San Carlo.

Although almost totally fatigued, she drew upon her reserves of energy to make her customary jaunty entry onto the stage of the Bellini. There, once more, she was greeted rapturously by a packed audience consisting of representatives from the Army, the Navy and the Royal Air Force. With a broad smile on her face, a wink of the eye and a high-pitched whistle she burst out" Well lads, I made it"! That she had enough strength to whistle amazed those who knew what she had endured in the previous hours of that evening. Her shrill whistle was the introduction to her own 'Gracie Fields ' special performance which was to last a further forty minutes.

In all she sang about a half-dozen songs, including the favourite, 'Sally'. She told a score or more jokes – each having the audience rolling in laughter. She playfully teased her audience too so that the hours of waiting was soon forgotten. After her rendition of 'Take me to Your Heart' she left the stage with a momentous ovation ringing in her ears.

After she had completed her performance at the Bellini theatre Gracie still had time and strength to pause outside the theatre. She responded enthusiastically to the goodwill wishes of the crowds waiting there and she stopped to sign many autographs. A little time after the crowds had dispersed she managed to pause to drink a small glass of whisky. Slowly sipping the same she is reported to have mused whimsically "Ive' got a terrible cold coming on. But believe me that would not have stopped me from doing my bit for the lads". Her 'bit' of course had demanded almost superhuman dedication. It came as only a small surprise to us that a special party was laid on for her after the show. During this occasion she was warmly congratulated by a series of high ranking officers before the demands of her schedule finally exhausted her and she took her leave to return to her hotel around 11.30pm. It was not surprising to hear the reaction to her deeds being summarised by the words in the mouths of many admirers "What a day, what a Gal"!

Gracie Fields

Gracie was a British comedienne who's Lancashire humour helped boost the morale of working class audiences throughout the depression years of the 1930's.

She was born in Rochdale in the year 1898 and named Grace Stansfield.

Her stage career started in 1911 and continued until the early 1950's.

She went to live in semi-retirement on the Isle of Capri, but was always delighted to greet tourists from Britain and would, at the drop of a hat, give impromptu performances for them.

She made many films and sang many hundreds of songs during her long and illustrious career the most notable was "Sally" a song which was especially associated with her.

She had a very distinctive voice with tremendous range and, although her humour was geared to the North of England, it was however, enjoyed by the whole country.

Her magic came from being completely natural, combined with a real affection, and love for her audience, she was never happier than when she was making people laugh In my opinion there has never been anybody quite like
"Our Gracie"
This grand old lady passed away in September 1979
God Bless Her

Chapter Eleven

The Legacy of Demobilisation, 1946

Gracie Field's and many other famous 'stars' – by their sheer presence amongst our troops – had uplifted us in a most singular fashion. Like many of my colleagues I felt I owed an inestimable personal debt to those 'Show Biz Troopers' who had personally entertained us whilst we were at the battle-fronts of the War. Gracie's contribution to our morale in that winter of 1945 certainly helped us to think more about the future and give strength to our hopes for 1946. As it turned out – with the War ending in the former year – the large-scale demobilisation of our Workshop Units in Italy started in January 1946.

Though it was bitterly cold throughout January in 1945, I still felt a new surge of optimism when, on 16th. I first saw my orders regarding demobilisation pinned on a notice board in the workshop barracks. When I headed to the Palace NAFFI as soon as possible to 'celebrate' I still had to undergo a medical test before my 'great escape' from army life. On the 1st. February I joined with the other soldiers in Group 26 to start the processing procedure to enable us to leave. The waiting period to leave Naples seemed interminable. I was unsure of the exact date I was to leave because I was ordered to go to Caserta, on the 3rd. February, to undertake canteen duties at our Divisional Headquarters. By now I realised, that my specialised battlefield and maintenance duties on armoured weapons were no longer required by the British Army.

Just over a week later, on 11th. February, I made one of my last visits in Army uniform to the San Carlo Opera House. I will never forget the performance of one of my favourite singers Ferruccio Tagliani in the production of Manon. I had recordings made by him in my home musical collection. On the following day I and fellow members of my Group 26 left for Lammie Camp but I was still able to make my last visit that evening to the San Carlo. Though 'Mefistofele' was the title of the production I had at last began to realise that those devilish 'evil spirits' of the Second World War had at last been extinguished.

One week later, at Naples, I was to board the 7pm. train – popularly known as the Medlock Special by our troops – to begin the return journey to Dear Old Blighty. My high spirits of excited expectancy were somewhat dampened on the following day. Having travelled throughout the night I arrived in Rome, at the main railway station, about 6am. Whilst moving through the throngs of people assembled there I had my large army pack stolen. Inside the pack was my gold watch, my greatcoat and one of my proudest possessions, viz., a Ziess Super Inkonta camera which I had used to take my innumerable war-time photographs. After this 'unholy' experience in the Holy City I moved on in melancholy mood to take supper in the seaside resort of Rimini, at 10pm.

Any lingering hopes of recovering my possessions finally disappeared when I was instructed to travel to Milan Central Station, to arrive there on the 21st. Outside the railway station, I took a tram-car to the assigned Number 20 Army Assembly Centre. I was to have only a short stay at the Centre. This, still permitted me to make a short tour of nearby historic Venice – the City famous for canals. My 'stop-over' in Milan lasted four days in all. On the 26th., after another early start to the day, my colleagues and I left Milan Central Station at 8am. and we moved on to Domodossola for a meal.

The following morning my Italian 'exile' came to end as I travelled by train through the famous Simplon Tunnel into Switzerland. By the evening I had reached Calais, in France, where I stayed at 212 Camp overnight.

The cost of losing my greatcoat was now to prove considerable. At 9.30am on 28th February I was happy enough to board one of the numerous troop-carrying cross Channel ferryboats bound for

Dover. There was no 'taxi ride' for us back to Aldershot however. Like thousands of others in our 'victorious army' I was taken in an open-lorry which was a source of extreme discomfort on that coatless Winter's day. How glad I was when my journey ended with shivering body and chattering teeth at 5pm.

Within a matter of days my whole life was to be changed in an unrecognisable fashion. On 1st March I and the colleagues I had lived alongside for several years were quickly rushed through a demobilisation procedure. Once this had been undertaken we went to the clothing store and were each given an ill-fitting civilian suit. How curious we must have looked dressed in these garments for most of us had forgotten how to wear a heavy civilian two-piece suit. I felt a little 'lost', therefore, as I took a train to London's Victoria Station, and then moved on to Euston where I finally headed north and arrived in Liverpool's Lime Street Station. Though my emotions were extremely unsettled as I dashed to find a Number 19 tramcar home I soon believed as I boarded the vehicle that this was to-date the happiest moment of my life.

The sheer relief at arriving safely home – after so many years away – was unforgettable. As fortune would have it I was soon to realise, after impulsively questioning my mother, sister and brother, that none of my relatives or friends had been killed or seriously injured. This had not been so for many others in Liverpool who were less fortunate than I.

The physical appearance of my home seaport had movingly altered. There were now many desolate open spaces, or 'wastelands' that often exhibited the ruined and damaged, bombed-out buildings. This desolation had affected many of those Liverpudlians who still lived there. Though the famous Liverpool or Scouse humour still surfaced in street corner conversations there were also periods of muted silence that markedly fell into the talk of those who spoke of their 'Blitz ' experiences of May 1941. The general atmosphere was one of happiness and relief but the guarded joy of many in their work places after the War seemed to arise from the widespread knowledge that many Liverpudlians had been struck in their hearts by paying the highest of prices for involvement in such a far-reaching scale of devastation.

For my part I had been absent from Liverpool during the darkest hours of those nerve-racking bombing raids of 1941. However, though I had been 'globe-trotting' with the trouble-shooting boys of the British Army's Fifth Division I had not been on a holiday. Whenever asked my colleagues and I were able to convey, if somewhat reluctantly, the details of our traumatic war-time experiences.

There were many of us who had no option but to undertake the arduous journeys to South Africa and through India, Iraq and Persia. They had also placed their lives at risk when – together with other units of the Eighth Army – they had made the amphibious assault landings in Sicily in 1943. After almost a year of intense fighting in Italy we had also helped to liberate Rome, in June 1944, from the Nazi stranglehold. Together with those who landed in Normandy, D Day 6th. June 1944, we had helped to strike a decisive blow in the struggle to return Europe to its democratic freedoms.

Hopefully my diaries and photographic records will help to keep alive some of the sacrifices that many thousands of my generation – back home and overseas – had to make during those dark, war-time days. Whenever a commemorative occasion, such as that in 1993 to mark the fiftieth anniversary of the Battle of the Atlantic, is undertaken my former comrades-in-arms and myself will remember those who did not return from their travels. Whenever occasions for thanksgiving, such as those in 1995 to celebrate fifty years of freedom in Europe, are undertaken we will rejoice but also keep in our minds those who did not return.

We also live in hope that the democratic freedoms won some fifty years before will be suitably cherished by generations younger than our own. Importantly, too, we live in hope that they will have a suitable regard for all those who sacrificed so much to obtain them. My above account, involving true-life adventure, historical fact and army life humour, is my own special tribute to them.

Our Legacy

We remember old comrades who rest
            forever far across the seas
Our cherished memories we share in
            their lonely graves
As each new generation passes by
Time will serve to enrich their names
            and deeds
When the sun rises in the morning
            and sets in the evening

We shall remember them with pride

Appendix

Principal routes of the journey

SOUTH AFRICA.

Scotland - Gourock
South Africa - Freetown.
  Durban.
  Madagascar.

INDIA.

  Nasik.
  Khaleitat.
  Mhow.
  Biaora.
  Shivpuri.
  Jhamsi -
  Alex Barracks.
  Cawnpore.
  Allahabad.
  Benares.
  Aurangabad.
  Hazaribagh.
  Ranchi
(return journey)
  Haziaribagh.
  Benares.
  Allahabad.
  Cawnpore.
  Pewar.
  Agra.
  Biaora.
  Mhow.
  Dulia.
  Nasik.
  Bombay.
(SS Varela to Basra).

PERSIAN GULF

  Basra. (Desert Camp).
  Khanjadwal.
  Baghdad.
  Kanaquin.
  Paitak Pass.
  Kermanshah.

Shah Pass.
Qum
Tehran
Malaya. (town)
Hamadan.
Kanaquin City.

IRAQ.

  Baghdad.
  Wadi Muhammadi.
  Rutba.
  Nathanya.

SYRIA.

  Qatana.
  Damascus.
  Beirut.

PALESTINE

  Haifa.
  Tel Aviv.
  Gaza.

EGYPT.

  Ismalia.
  Zagazz-Benha.
  Tanta.
  Damahul - El. Amira.
  El. Alamein.
  Alexandria

**Route taken from
invasion of Sicily to Anzio**

SICILY.

  Avola.
  Cassibile.
  Syracuse.
  Belvedere.
  Priola.

Melilli.
Augusta.
Villa Samundo.
Catania.
Lentini.
Gerbini.
Catania
Misterbianco.
Paterno.
Belpasso.
Nicolosi.
Pedara.
Trescastagni.
Acireale.

ITALY.

  Palmi.
  Rossano.
  Monteleoni.
  Nicastro.
  Amantea.
  Paola.
  Montalto
  Cetraro.
  Belvedere.
  San Sosti.
  Scalea.
  Maratea.
  Treconina.
  Lauria.
  Lagonegro.
  Montesano.
  Sala Consalina.
  Padua.
  Brienza.
  Picerno.
  Castel Grande.
  Potenza.
  Tolve.
  Irsina.
  Spinazzola.
  Minervino.

Canosa.
Foggia.
Lucera.
San Severo.
Seracapriola.
San Croce.
Bonefro.
Casacalenda.
Ferrazzano.
Bojano.
Isernia.
Cantalupo.
Biaro.
Borella.
San Angelo.
Palmoli.
Gissi.
Casalaguida.
Lanciano.
Torino-Di-Sangro.
Vasto.
Termoli.
Serracapriola.
San Severo.
Lucera.
Ariano.
Grottaminarda.
Avelino.
Monteforte.
Cicciano.
Cancello.
San Giuliano
Mignano.
Mondragone.
Pozzuoli .
Anzio.
Rome.

L. A. D. Personnel
India - Iraq - Persia - Syria
- Sicily - Italy

A.S.M. Gilmour -
  (Replaced by) A.S.M.
  Sherriff.
Sergeant Frank Ainsworth
  (Mechanic).
Corporal Fred Thurgood -
  (Mechanic).
L. Corporal Jim Gonzales
  (Myself, Electrician).
L. Corporal Howard Narra
  (Stores).
CFN George Dalloway
  (Welder).
CFN Bill Wignall
  (Don R. Cum Cook).
CFN Doug Tabard
  (Fitter).
CFN Len Beyer
  (Driver).
CFN Bob Naylor
  Driver).
CFN Frank Tack
  Driver).
CFN Bill Cox
  Driver).

Armed Units

Carpathian Division
Commandos
18th Light Anti-Aircraft
  egiment
15th Infantry Brigade
5th Bn. The
  Reconnaissance Corps
1st Bn. The Green
  Howards
1st Bn. The York and
  Lancaster Regiment
1st Bn. The Kings Own
  Yorkshire Light Infantry
4th Parachute regiment
45th American
  Reconnaissance unit
Gurkhas
Herman Goering Panzer
  Division
Light Air Detatchment
The Royal Regiment of
  Artillery
9th Field Regiment
91st Field Regiment
92nd Field Regiment
156th Field Regiment
Rangers Bn.
Royal Engineers
Royal Ulster Rifles
2nd Bn. The Royal
  Iniskilling Fusiliers
13th Infantry Brigade

Subscribers

A Allen N. Mr

B Ball F. W. Mr
Ball Grahame Mr
Baker Frank
Baker James Edward
Baker Keith
Bell Jack
Bird J. Mrs
Biggin K. Mr
Boak F. E. Mr. E.A.V.A
Bride S. Mrs
Brooks P. K. Miss

C Calder Stan
Church Paul
Cooke S. D. Miss
Cosgrove Ron Mr
Craven Mark E.
Critchell H. G. 2Lt RAOC

D Davies Oliver W.
Deeprose Maurice Mr
Dodd D. B.
Douglas J. Dr.

E Ellis F. Mr
Evans Peter

F Fagan Leslie Mr
Ford Charles Mr

G Garner C. Mr
Gardiner Valerie
Gavin Arthur

H Harris P.G. Capt. MC
Hawtree Raymond M. M.
Hodson M. W. Mr
Holt J. A. Mr
Howard Gloria Mrs
Hughes Gordon

J Jeremiah W. Mr
Jones Donald Mr

K Kaye H. M.
Kendrick Geoff.
Knowles E. L. Mr

L Lenhan Frank Adrian
Lowe Joe

M MacDonald L. J. Mr
McCormick Herbert Mr
McNally Chev, James N. K. W, I.M.O.S.
Meakin F. S.
Michael R. C. Ex Kings Liverpool
Molloy Michael B. A.
Mumford Sidney G.

N Neuss M E Miss

O Oliver Charles M.

P Parkinson J. C.
Parkinson John L.
Pearson C. E. J
Pemberton Beatrice
Potter Sydney

R Russell Eric James
Ryan John H.

S Sandiford R. Mr
Scott John P.
Smallwood Charles
Southern Roy
Swanson Ronald

T Taylor Brian
Tilson Angus
Tupman A. Mr
Tweedle M.
Tyrell E. Mr

W Welch G. A. Dr.
White (Chalkie) Stan
Williams N. J. Mr
Woolfenden F. Ex Kings Liverpool
Wyatt Milton

Y Yates W. E.

Index